Table of Contents

Exploring County Durham.................................2
The Queen on Tour...18
Mr Bean Telly Classic..22
The Founding of the NHS.................................26
10 Beautiful British Libraries............................34
Great British Icons: Wedgewood......................44
Lady Mary Montagu..48
London's Savile Row..52
The Vulcan Bomber...60
The Slang Page...64

About the Magazine

The Anglotopia Magazine is published quarterly by Anglotopia LLC, a USA registered Corporation. All contents copyrighted and may not be reproduced without permission.

Letters to the Editors may be sent via email to: info@anglotopia.net

Photos: Cover: Dunrobin Castle, Scotland, This Page: The Monument in the City of London, Back Cover: Snowdrops, Dorset, Inside Back Cover: Hardknott Roman Fort, Cumbria

EXPLORING COUNTY DURHAM
A Jewel of the North

By Laura Porter

We made it as far as Leeds in West Yorkshire for Anglotopia issue #10, but let's go further up the country and explore Durham in the North East of England.

The county has breathtaking scenery and award-winning attractions. It's great for city breaks, heritage tours, coastal holidays, and countryside escapes. Plus the Anglotopia Publisher, Jonathan, can lay claim to having ancestry from the region so I knew it was time to get to know the area better.

To assuage confusion, the region and the city you are probably most likely to have heard of here are both called Durham. Durham City (also called the county town) has the famous Cathedral and a UNESCO World Heritage Site. The region, County Durham, includes the Durham Dales that form part of the North Pennines Area of Outstanding Natural Beauty (AONB), the Vale of Durham's stunning landscape in an area that was a world leader in the country's industrial development, and the Durham Coast with its wild and beautiful coastline.

PRONUNCIATION

Locals bring the two syllables together, so it sounds more like 'Derm', but other parts of England pronounce Durham as 'Du-rerm'.

GETTING THERE

Durham is 270 miles north of London. Travelling by train is much faster than driving as it's a three-hour train ride from King's Cross. You know you have reached Durham when, from the East Coast railway line, you see the Cathedral set grandly on a rocky promontory – one of the best welcoming views to any city.

Newcastle Airport is served by regular domestic and international flights and Teesside International Airport has connections to New York via Amsterdam.

GETTING AROUND

Durham is a relatively small city and driving in the city centre is discouraged with a congestion charge. There is a Park & Ride bus, and the Cathedral Bus service links the rail station, city centre and Durham Cathedral and Castle.

For exploring the county, it is best to hire a car, and there is plenty of availability from Durham City.

DURHAM CITY

Cobbled streets, a winding river and prominent peninsula, Durham is a very attractive small city with one of the most recognisable landmarks in the UK. Since 1986, Durham Cathedral, together with the adjacent Durham Castle, has been designated a UNESCO World Heritage site.

Durham Cathedral

Described by Bill Bryson as 'the best Cathedral on planet Earth', building Durham Cathedral began in 1093 and it is dedicated to the Saxon Saint Cuthbert (c.634-87) who was one of the most popular saints in early medieval England. His tomb was moved from Lindisfarne in 793 when the Holy Island suffered England's first ever Viking raid. After journeying across the North with his body and relics, the monks settled in Durham in 995. Then when William the Conqueror made a pilgrimage to Durham, he decided to build Cuthbert a new home.

Also buried here are the remains of The Venerable Bede, a monk who lived in the 7th and 8th century who was responsible for the system we use today when counting the years forward or backwards from the year of Christ's birth: AD and BC.

Much admired for its Romanesque architecture, Durham Cathedral is a popular filming location. The cloisters – the most intact set of medieval buildings in England to have survived the Reformation – became the snow-covered quadrangle for 'Harry Potter and the Philosopher's Stone' (UK) / 'Harry Potter and the Sorcerer's Stone' (US) and the scene of Ron's slug vomiting in 'The Chamber of Secrets'. The Chapter House was the setting for Professor McGonagall's class when she taught the young wizards to turn animals into water goblets. And the south side of the triforium, part of the upper

levels in the Nave, was the setting for the forbidden corridor guarded by Fluffy the three-headed dog. The Chapter House and triforium are not open to the public, but the cloisters are open daily and free to visit. Durham Cathedral was also featured in the second highest-grossing film of all time, the 2019 blockbuster 'Avengers: Endgame' when the Galilee Chapel and the South Nave Aisle were used as part of Asgard.

TOP TIP

Durham Cathedral is open every day but do check for special services before visiting as it can affect access.

While the Cathedral is free to visit (donation suggested), there is a charge to see Open Treasure. It is worth it alone to see the main gallery as it is a magnificent 14th-century monks' dormitory – the only surviving monastic dormitory in the UK. Open Treasure explores the story of Durham Cathedral plus the people and history as well as tracing the development of Christianity from Roman times to the present day. Photos are not allowed of the exhibits, but you can take a photo of yourself dressed as a monk.

Linking with the regional 'Year of Pilgrimage 2020', Open Treasure will have an exhibition exploring the history of pilgrimage and how it was experienced at Durham before and after the Reformation. ('Pilgrimage' is on from 19 May to 12 September 2020.)

After enjoying the Cathedral's spectacular rib-vaulted Nave, and admiring the medieval clock, the beautiful organ from the Romantic era of England, and the exquisite 18th century rose window, why not climb the Central Tower? It reopened in 2019 after extensive conservation works, and it is 325 steps to reach the top. Slightly less strenuous is the climb to the top of the North West Tower at only 137 steps. Both offer wonderful views of Durham City and beyond.

COOL TIP

The rose window was made by Clayton & Bell of London in 1876 and is over 28 feet across. You can make your own stained glass window (on a smaller scale!) at the nearby Crushed Chilli Gallery.

And before you leave, do see the scale representation of Durham Cathedral in the Undercroft. It is the largest LEGO model ever built by the general public. It contains 300,000 bricks and was a fundraiser for the Cathedral (£1 per brick).

DID YOU KNOW?

As well as the impressive Cathedral, Durham City has a further seventeen churches to explore.

Durham Castle

Also originally built in the 11th century on the order of William the Conqueror, Durham Castle was an imposing fortress that later became a lavish palace for the Bishops of Durham. It is now a Grade I listed building, an accredited museum, part of the World Heritage Site, and home to University College, the founding college of Durham University.

Durham Castle is open to the general public to visit but only through guided tours since it is in use as a working building and is home to over 100 students.

TOP TIP

Stand on Prebends Bridge, over the River Wear, to get the best view of the Castle and Cathedral for photos.

Durham Museum

This local history museum is housed in a historic church close to the Cathedral. It describes the development of the city from the 17th century to today.

Wharton Park

This is a gem in the heart of Durham with commanding views over the city. At its summit, there are Grade II listed battlements dating back to 1858. John Ruskin, a 19th-century philosopher, described the spectacular views as "the Eighth Wonder of the World".

Crook Hall & Gardens

The 13th century Grade I listed medieval hall is a wonderful backdrop to the idyllic English gardens nestled in the heart of Durham City. Open all year round; it is set in four acres with two walled gardens, a maze, a silver and white garden, and a Shakespeare garden.

SHOPPING TIP

Durham market hall is the oldest indoor market. It is more like an independent department store than a market and home to around 50 traders.

Durham Oriental Museum

Devoted to the art and archaeology of the great cultures of North Africa and Asia, this university museum is the only museum of its kind in Northern England. Where else can you see Ancient Egyptian mummies, Chinese porcelain, Japanese woodblock prints, and head-hunting swords from Borneo under the same roof?

Durham Botanic Gardens

Take time to wander through the Alpine Garden, Winter Garden, Bamboo Grove, Woodland Garden, and wildflower meadow. There is no need to rush, as there are lots of places to stop and enjoy the space. Don't miss the glasshouses, especially the tropical rainforest house where there's a button to make it rain.

EVENING TIP

The Gala Theatre has touring theatre productions and local talent from the North East, plus comedy, talks, music, and screenings.

Where to eat in Durham City

Cafédral is a family-run independent cafe that's great for lunch, and Flat White Café has amazing coffee and homemade pastries. Vennels is the oldest restaurant in the city, and Zen has recommended Thai food. The Rabbit Hole has dim sum in an opulent 1920s inspired Shanghai Supper Club, and Cosy Club has an outdoor terrace overlooking the river. Claypath Deli uses local ingredients to produce Mediterranean dishes, and Bells Fish shop serves proper fish and chips. Cafe on the Green has the best cheese scones, I'm told.

Outstanding Art Lounge Bar is great for art and cocktails, and the Tin of Sardines gin bar has over 300 gins on the menu. Speaking of gin, when I was in the city I heard that Durham Gin is planning a visitor attraction under the river, so that's one to be aware of.

Where to Stay in Durham City

The Radisson Blu Hotel is overlooking the River Wear in the city centre and Durham Marriott Hotel Royal County has an indoor pool. Hotel Indigo is in a heritage building and has a gorgeous marble staircase. The Kingslodge Inn is considered a traditional country pub in the city with free parking, and the Victoria pub is rated four-star accommodation in a Grade II listed Victorian Inn.

VALE OF DURHAM

The Vale of Durham surrounds the city and has been shaped by the county's rich social and industrial past. In the 18th and 19th centuries, Northern England was a world leader in industrial innovation and enterprise, and Durham was at the forefront of these dramatic changes. The county's industrial development was based on coal and iron and the need to carry both to markets which led to major innovations that revolutionised transport throughout the world.

Today there is stunning countryside making it perfect for long walks or bike rides, revealing unforgettable views across the county.

Beamish – The Living Museum of the North

I had wanted to visit Beamish for a long time, so this was a real highlight as it brings history to life. It's not one building but, instead, a collection of heritage buildings made into small towns so you can buy a bag of broken biscuits and carbolic soap at the Co-op grocers, or enjoy coal-fired fish and chips from Davy's Fried Fish shop.

Spread over 300 acres, the museum's guiding principle is to preserve an example of everyday life in urban and rural North East England at the climax of industrialisation in the early 20th century. It's so well done, Beamish was used as a filming location for the 2019 'Downton Abbey' movie.

You catch a tram or heritage bus to each location – do admire the countryside views from the top deck – and everyone working on-site is dressed in clothes of the era. They can answer questions so ask about remedies in the chemist or baking tips at Herron's Bakery. It's proper hands-on history at this immersive attraction.

In the 1900s town, you can wander into the dentist's and then buy handmade confectionery in the sweet shop – cinder toffee (honeycomb) is recommended. See the printer at work, learn about old money in the bank, then stop at The Sun Inn pub where you can buy a decent pint before having your portrait taken in the Edwardian photographers' studio.

At the Pit Village, you can go into the school, chapel, and homes before heading to the colliery for a guided tour down the drift mine. Yes, you can go into a real coal mine! You won't want to stay long though as you have to remain hunched over and it's pretty dark, but you will have a newfound respect for the men who spent hours down there every day.

Open all year round; you could easily spend a full day at Beamish and still not see it all. I heard Christmas at Beamish is magical, so there are many reasons to return.

HOTEL TIP

Beamish Hall Hotel is a classic country house hotel nearby so you could stay close and have a couple of days exploring Beamish. And, an 18th-century coaching inn at Beamish itself is opening soon so you will be able to stay overnight on-site.

Locomotion

The Vale of Durham became the cradle of the railways. The North East of England has had a colliery since the 15th century and railways were built to haul coal. But it was here on 27 September 1825 that the world's first public passenger steam railway began its maiden journey in Shildon. A full-size replica of Locomotion No.1 can be seen at this family-friendly attraction that is home to over 70 vehicles from the National Collection.

The museum looks at railway development, passenger and goods transportation, and historic buildings. You can see King Edward VII and Queen Alexandra's train and her carriage, and the shop has some excellent Harry Potter and Thomas the Tank Engine merchandise.

Supported by the Science Museum Group, Locomotion is open daily and is free to visit.

TOP TIP

The car park is a short walk from the site, but you will know you are at the right place as you walk alongside a disused railway line.

Auckland Project

Bishop Auckland has the Auckland Project bringing changes to this sleepy market town. Start your visit at the Auckland Tower where you can buy tickets for the attractions and go up to the 15-meter viewing platform to see the estate of Auckland Castle including a deer park and lush rural landscape beyond. Then head to Auckland Castle to see the multi-million-pound conservation and refurbishment.

This 900-year-old former home of the Prince Bishops of Durham is one of the best-preserved medieval Bishops' palaces in Europe. The power and privileges the Prince Bishops held within the region were equal to the kings across the rest of the country. Gifted immense secular powers after the Norman conquest by the king, they could raise their own army, mint their own coins, increase taxes, and maintain the law between the Tyne and Tees. The Bishops of Durham still sit in the House of Lords and represent the region.

The core 14th and 16th-century structures have been reworked, and the earliest part is the medieval Great Hall. You can see the largest private chapel in Europe, and the State Rooms and Bishop's private apartments have been returned to their Gothic splendour. Within the Castle, admire the art at Bishop Trevor Gallery; many also come for the views out of the windows and to see the building as well as the art.

Back in the Market Place, the Mining Art Gallery was much better than expected. Empowered by social reform between the First and Second World Wars, miners began to express their experiences and feelings through art. The Gallery shares emotive tales of the trials and tribulations of the county's coal-mining past. I found it a really emotional visit as I never really understood the impact of the coal mine closures in the 1980s.

Inspired by Francisco de Zurbarán's series of paintings, 'Jacob and his Twelve Sons', which hang in Auckland Castle's Long Dining Room, a dedicated Spanish Art Gallery opened in 2020. County Durham is home to the UK's largest collection of Spanish art outside London. Another reason to stay longer will be the Spanish restaurant opening too.

Also opening in 2020, an extension on Auckland Castle will house the Faith Museum with ten galleries exploring how faith has shaped lives and communities, and how belief has been a driving force throughout the history of Britain and Ireland. The 17th-century Walled Garden and its new restaurant will also open in 2020.

ACCOMMODATION TIP

Bradley Burn Farm has holiday cottages and a chalet holiday park with a recommended farm shop and cafe.

Kynren

You really could spend a full day in Bishop Auckland in the summer months as Kynren is an epic 90-minute open-air theatrical show telling the story of England. It starts at dusk and ends with an incredible firework display. Described as a 'thrilling romp through British history', over 1,000 cast and crew perform on a magnificent 7.5-acre outdoor stage to time travel with you through 2,000 years of history, myth, and legend.

Kynren is the reason I booked a trip to the North East, and it was as brilliant as I had hoped. You follow Arthur, the son of a mining family, on his spellbinding journey through time and watch legends come to life. There are battles between Boudicca and the Romans, then Vikings and Anglo-Saxon leaders. Daring knights joust on horseback, and Queen Elizabeth I floats in on her royal barge in conversation with Shakespeare. The choreographed cast of all ages (including animals!) walk on water and bring history to life. I still have no idea how a Viking ship, complete with Vikings on board, appeared out of the water and then sank down again.

You will see the lavish celebrations of Queen Victoria's Diamond Jubilee before the world wars and right up to today. You won't be surprised to hear that Kynren performances regularly command a standing ovation.

TOP TIP

Kynren is on Saturdays from late June to mid-September. It's great for all ages.

Binchester Roman Fort

Close to Bishop Auckland, see the impressive remains of the Commandant's house and the

neighbouring bath-house containing one of the best-preserved examples of a hypocaust (underfloor heating system) in the whole of Britain.

Diggerland

If you are either bringing the kids or are a big kid yourself, head to the Diggerland theme park to ride, drive, and operate real full-size construction machinery.

Durham County Cricket Club

Time your visit between May and September, and you can enjoy world-class cricket in the area too.

HOTEL TIP

A great base to explore the Vale of Durham is Thomas Wright House in Byers Green. It has eight bedrooms named after constellations with one boasting a private terrace and hot tub. They also have two holiday cottages, with hot tubs, available as well. I stayed at Thomas Wright House and can highly recommend it. The restaurant is loved by locals too. Or if you would like to be near a golf course, Ramside Hall Hotel, Golf and Spa is a stunning four-star hotel, and there is even treehouse accommodation on offer.

DURHAM DALES

To the west of Durham City, and covering half the county, are the Durham Dales. Made up of Teesdale, an area hewn by glacial movements during Ice Age Britain and split by the River Tees, and Weardale, whose history and heritage is founded on lead mining. The Dales form part of the North Pennines Area of Outstanding Natural Beauty, the second largest AONB in the country and also a European and UNESCO Global Geopark. The area is recognised as the darkest mainland AONB in the country with more dark sky discovery sites than anywhere else in England.

The landscape of moors and hills, waterfalls, and meandering rivers has inspired artists and writers throughout the ages.

Bowes Museum

Housing internationally significant collections of fine and decorative arts, the Museum was purpose-built in the 19th century by wealthy businessman John Bowes and his French actress wife, Joséphine. (John Bowes has a royal connection as his uncle was the great-great-grandfather of Her Majesty Queen Elizabeth The Queen Mother, 1900-2002.) The couple were unable to have children so enjoyed buying beautiful things. They were relatively thrifty as few items were over £10, yet they purchased 15,000 objects between 1862 and 1874. They decided to build a museum for the people with their collections and used French architect Jules Pellechet who created this magnificent French-style chateau. The vast, grand, and notably symmetrical Bowes Museum opened in 1892.

Paintings by Van Dyck, Goya, Canaletto, Gainsborough, and other Old Masters can be found in impressive galleries alongside textiles, dress, silver, ceramics, and furniture as well as the unique Silver Swan musical automaton. This came from James Cox's museum in London in 1774, and it is turned on at 2 pm daily. You don't want to miss the mesmerising Silver Swan so be in the gallery by 1.45 pm and get a spot near the head for the best views. The performance only takes 32 seconds, but it is beautiful to see.

NEARBY

As well as the farm shop, Cross Lanes Organic Farm has an organic kitchen that serves speciality dishes using fresh, local, and seasonal ingredients.

Raby Castle

You may have already seen Raby Castle without knowing as it was a filming location for 'Victoria' in 2016. One of the finest medieval castles in England, it was built in the 14th century by the powerful Neville family. It started as a family-owned manor house (converted from a training school for soldiers), was then owned by the Crown, and since 1626 Raby Castle has been the seat of Lord and

Lady Barnard of the Vane family.

The Castle was home to Cicely Neville, Rose of Raby, mother of Kings Edwards IV and Richard III. (Edward IV was the first Yorkist king from 1461. Cicely was a great-great-grand aunt to Catherine Parr, the sixth wife of her great-grandson Henry VIII.) Raby Castle was also the scene where the 'Rising of the North' plot took place and served as a Parliamentary stronghold during the civil war.

The grandeur of the Castle rooms reminded me of Buckingham Palace. The Grand Entrance has many stag heads on the walls from the 250-acre deer park surrounding the Castle, and the ceiling was raised to allow carriages to drive right inside. The Baron's Hall has 5,000 books on the walls and is the longest room in the North of England at 132 feet.

Raby Castle is open from March to September, with an additional opening for Christmas when Santa Claus is in residence.

TOP TIP

Guided tours are usually available in the afternoon so spend the morning exploring the park and gardens.

High Force Waterfall

This is one of England's most impressive waterfalls. The River Tees suddenly and spectacularly drops 21 meters over the Whin Sill rock into a plunge pool below.

High Force is surrounded by the stunning countryside of Upper Teesdale and is situated in the North Pennines AONB. It's home to an abundance of animal and plant wildlife throughout the seasons from the vast array of wildflowers, ferns, and towering trees, to Roe deer and otters.

From Bowlees Visitor Centre there is a gentle woodland walk to lead you to a viewing area at the base of the waterfall. Summerhill Force and Gibson's Cave is a half-mile in the opposite direction and also worth seeing.

HOTEL TIP

High Force Hotel is a traditional country inn near Raby Castle and High Force Waterfall. Set in the picturesque setting of Upper Teesdale, the dog-friendly hotel makes a great base for exploring the area.

Killhope Lead Mining Museum

Killhope is a multi-award winning 19th-century mining museum in the centre of the North Pennines AONB, where you can experience the life and work of the lead mining families of the region.

HOTEL TIP

Headlam Hall Hotel and Spa is an idyllic 17th-century country house hotel surrounded by its own rolling farmland. The period features reflect the rural heritage of the property, and the indoor pool is welcome after a day of country walks.

DURHAM COAST

On the far east of the county, this dramatic stretch of heritage coastline is rugged yet stunning. It's a stretch of wild and beautiful coast reclaimed from the heavy industry of coal mining to offer beaches, clifftop walks, and coastal charm.

Magnificent sweeps of magnesian grassland along the cliffs support a mix of plants, insects, and several colonies of rare northern brown argus butterfly. Exposed rocky shores at low tide reveal returning marine life, sea urchins, and anemones, and birds along the coast include skylarks, sanderling, purple sandpipers, and not forgetting the annual visitor from West Africa, the little tern which nests at Crimdon each year.

It wasn't always so clean as in 1991, Blast Beach in Seaham was used as a location for 'Alien 3'. It was chosen for the alien planet because the beach was so blackened by coal waste. This stretch of the Durham Coast was once home to the biggest coal mine in Europe. It became buried under two and a half million tonnes of colliery waste every year,

but thanks to a massive clean-up project the vast majority of the waste has now been removed, and wildlife and people are able to use the coast again.

Collect Sea Glass

While the main activity in this area is coastline walks, do stop to collect the brightly coloured sea glass washed up at Seaham. The abundance of glass left on Seaham's beaches (originating from the Londonderry Bottleworks factory which closed in 1921), has been smoothed by the force of the North Sea's waves. Spotting these gem-like pieces of Durham's heritage always raises a smile.

HOTEL TIP

Enjoy five-star luxury at Seaham Hall and Serenity Spa. The Grade II listed townhouse has a stunning clifftop location with a spa that draws influence from Far Eastern healing and wellness rituals.

AFTERNOON TEA

I know you would be disappointed if I didn't share my afternoon tea recommendations for Durham. The region produces delicious cheese scones so don't be surprised to find these on the cake stand. (2019 prices noted below.)

At The Bowes Museum, Cafe Bowes serves the best meal of the day from 2 pm to 4 pm daily (£15.95). The Stables Café at Raby Castle has afternoon tea (£27.50 for two) as well as cheese and fruit scones available. At Crook Hall & Gardens, afternoon tea is served in the Georgian Drawing Room or one of the gardens (£24.50). At Beamish, afternoon tea is served in the Cookson Room overlooking the 1900s Town with cakes from their own Herron's Bakery (£15, must book in advance). And the Undercroft Restaurant at Durham Cathedral has tea and cake delights too (£11.95, must book in advance).

Acknowledgements

We were fortunate to have the support of www.thisisdurham.com in planning the research trip for this article. Do use their website to find out more about all of the places mentioned here. LNER provided train tickets and, if travelling from London, we would definitely recommend them as the three-hour journey was smooth and direct.

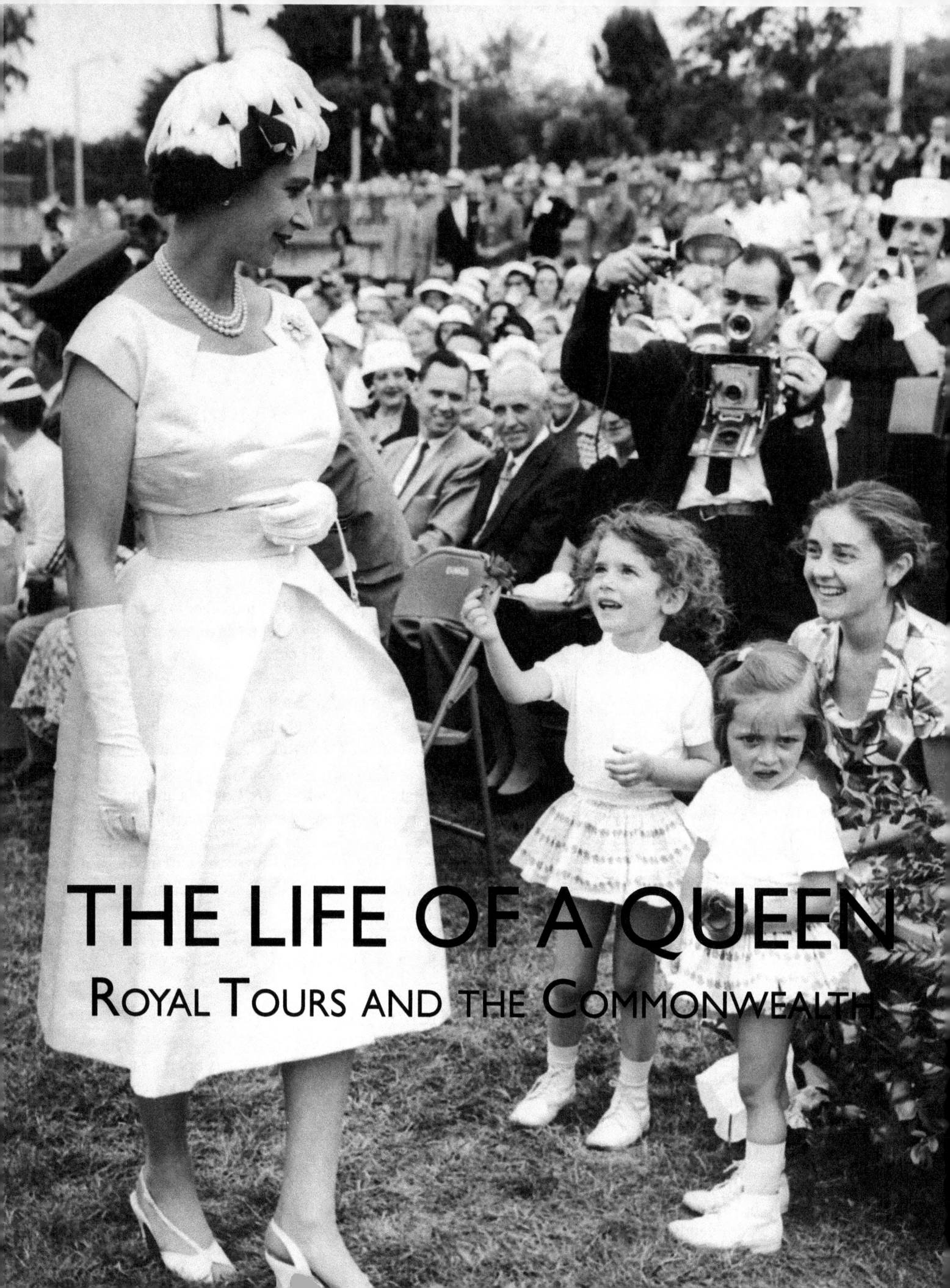

THE LIFE OF A QUEEN
ROYAL TOURS AND THE COMMONWEALTH

During her long reign, Queen Elizabeth has made more than 260 official overseas visits to over 116 countries around the world. She is the most traveled head of state by far. She is the first monarch to circle the globe yet she does not hold a passport—British passports are issued in the name of the Queen, so she really doesn't have any reason to issue one to herself in her own name, although the rest of the royal family have passports. She hardly needs an introduction when she travels, but years ago on a tour in Scotland, her host got tangled in his sword trying to get out of the car, so Elizabeth finally introduced herself, saying, "My Lord-Lieutenant appears to be having difficulty in getting out of the car, so I'd better introduce myself. I'm the Queen."

Elizabeth went on her first airplane flight in 1945, a trip to Northern Ireland with her parents. Six months later, she went on her first official visit without her parents.

Before her marriage to Philip, Elizabeth went on a royal tour to Africa with her sister Margaret and her parents, in 1947. The trip was a way to introduce Elizabeth to the Commonwealth, and while the month-long boat trip there and back was full of seasickness, the family had a wonderful time together as just "we four," as they liked to call themselves. Elizabeth got to see how her parents coped with the grueling schedule despite her father's failing health. She learned about race relations in South Africa and Rhodesia—knowledge and skills that would prove valuable to her later in her reign as these countries faced rebellions and unrest. In South Africa, Elizabeth celebrated her twenty-first birthday, with parties and a speech broadcast across the Commonwealth which she addressed to the young people who had suffered in the "terrible and glorious years of the second world war." She said for the first time what would become her message throughout her reign: "If we all go forward together with an unwavering faith, a high courage, and a quiet heart, we shall be able to make of this ancient Commonwealth an even grander thing--more free, more prosperous, more happy, and a more powerful influence for good in the world. I should like to make [a] dedication now. It is very simple. I declare before you all that my whole life whether it be long or short shall be devoted to your service and the service of our great imperial family to which we all belong."

Her father, King George VI, dedicated himself to the welfare of the Commonwealth, as well. The notion of the Commonwealth is a 20th-century invention to describe countries once in the Empire but now transitioning to independence while still keeping their link to the monarchy. No longer ruling colonies like in the 18th and 19th centuries or fighting the Spanish Armada and spreading across the world like Imperial Britain of the first Queen Elizabeth's reign, Queen Elizabeth II felt it was her duty to show compassion and guidance to the countries that once fell under Britain's rule. While she doesn't have executive power in the Commonwealth countries, she has a lot of influence, often being sent in (or choosing to send herself in) when she sees them needing a push in the right direction, or to pave the way for the Prime Minister to open discussions with their leaders. Philip calls her the "Commonwealth psychotherapist."

In 1951, before her accession to the throne, Elizabeth and Philip took a 35-day royal tour across Canada and the United States, learning their new roles as royal diplomats. Elizabeth told Charteris, her private secretary, "my face is aching from smiling." Philip, however, made a public joke about Canada being "a good investment" for the Crown.

That comment didn't get quite the same reception. Charteris explained it this way, saying Philip "was impatient. He hadn't yet defined his role . . . and sometimes, I think, felt that the Princess paid more attention to them than to him." One wonders how Philip thinks it could be otherwise. They would find their roles as the years went on, although Philip would still put his foot in his mouth fairly regularly. On a later tour of the Cayman Islands, Philip said, "aren't you all descended from pirates?" He also didn't suffer the press lightly, at one point responding to a question he didn't like with the remark, "damn fool question," and telling a group in the Caribbean, "you have mosquitos, I have the press."

And on one notable occasion when a member of the press asked how his flight was, Philip responded, "Have you ever flown in a plane?" "Oh yes sir, many times" "Well, it was just like that." Philip even had a name for it, given when he was speaking at a dental conference: "Dontopedalogy is the science of opening your mouth and putting your foot in it, a science which I have practiced a good many years."

HMY Britannia - Used on many tours

Elizabeth, on the other hand, rarely spoke a wrong word. When she visited Niagara Falls on the trip in 1951, she worried about the mist ruining her hair, saying "It looks very damp." And on a royal trip to Norway where she opened an art exhibition of giant nude sculptures, she said she made sure "I was not photographed between a pair of those great thighs." She was immensely popular on her royal tours, drawing huge crowds. On the trip to Washington in 1951, President Truman called her "a fairy princess," taken with her immediately. She had that effect on people. Plus she was dedicated, hard-working, and empathetic.

When a Canadian official thought Elizabeth might need a break, her secretary responded, "Her Majesty is trained for eight hours," and another staff member once said, "she's got very good legs, and she can stand for a long time . . . The Queen is tough as a yak."

While Elizabeth refuses to give interviews to the press, she does show the same compassion and dedication to them as she does to everyone else. When a member of the press was traveling with her entourage on a royal tour, and his wife went into labor back in London, it was clear that the journalist wasn't going to make it home in time on a commercial flight, so the Queen said, "that won't do at all, let him fly home with me on my royal flight."

November 1953 saw the start of a 43,000-mile royal tour for Elizabeth and Philip from Bermuda west through the Panama Canal on to Fiji then New Zealand and Australia where Elizabeth was the first reigning monarch to visit. During the three weeks on the boat, Elizabeth worked in her office daily but also spent a lot of time playing on deck with Philip and the staff. In Fiji she was a good sport about eating strange foods, in Tonga she was reunited with Queen Salote who had come to her coronation and been very popular. Elizabeth was a good sport again in Tonga when she had to sit on the floor and eat with her hands. All over the Pacific, Philip and Elizabeth were crowd-pleasers. Philip said, "The level of adulation, you wouldn't believe it, it could have been corroding. It would have been very easy to play to the gallery, but I took a conscious decision not to do that. Safer not to be too popular. You can't fall too far." Philip was also a great consolation to Elizabeth when the schedule got too tough, telling her, "don't look so sad, sausage." The couple then continued on from Australia to Ceylon (Sri Lanka), Uganda, and Libya, where Elizabeth had a hard time with the heat (as anyone would). The newly-finished royal yacht which Philip had helped design, Brittania, met them in Libya, with young Charles and Anne on board. After several months apart, the first reunion with the children was not as warm as Charles might have liked. Elizabeth had to greet the dignitaries on board first, telling Charles, "no, not you dear," something Charles would always remember. In private, however, the family had a great reunion, with Charles showing his parents all over the yacht that he'd already been traveling on for a week.

Philip goes on all of the royal tours with Elizabeth, the ones where he goes somewhere on his own raises eyebrows with the press and elicits comments about how their marriage must be in trouble. Elizabeth is always firm about how that is not the case.

Yet even when they are together, they sometimes fight like other couples. On one royal tour to Australia when the couple were heard fighting, Elizabeth later tells the staff, "I'm sorry for that little interlude, but as you know, it happens in every marriage." On a solo tour of Philip's in 1956 when he opened the Olympic Games in Melbourne and was gone for four months, rumors of trouble in the royal marriage were particularly rampant. To quell the gossip, Elizabeth and her staff met Philip on board the Brittania sporting false beards to match the ones Philip and the crew had grown.

On a royal tour to Canada in 1957, Elizabeth was the first monarch to open Canadian Parliament. She then went on to the U.S. to meet Eisenhower, who had been a great friend to her parents during World War II.

He went on to say, "You both have captivated the people of our country by your charm and graciousness."

She carried that graciousness on to a football game in Maryland (where she didn't understand the rules), and to an impromptu stop at a grocery store, where she commented to one mother shopping, "how nice that you can bring your children along." (She clearly didn't realize that most American moms would rather not bring their children along but rarely have a choice). The manager of the supermarket commented after she left, "it was the greatest thing that ever happened to me." Eisenhower later returned the visit with a visit of his own to Balmoral where Elizabeth cooked scones for him herself, sending him the recipe written by hand.

The Commonwealth was always very special to Elizabeth; she considers it her legacy. Countries that might have left the Commonwealth while in crisis stayed because of her influence. While on a royal tour to New Zealand in 1953, she gave her Christmas message from there, commenting "the Crown is not merely an abstract symbol of our unity but a personal and living bond between you and me." And in a Christmas message in 1957, Elizabeth addressed the Commonwealth, saying, "I cannot lead you into battle, but I can do something else. I can give you my heart, and my devotion to those old islands and to all the peoples of our brotherhood of nations." She had shown that devotion a year earlier in Nigeria, shaking hands with recovering lepers. In 1961 she went to Ghana to try to keep the country in the Commonwealth even though they had already declared their independence. It was a dangerous trip, not recommended by her advisers, but her response was, "How silly I should look if I was scared to visit Ghana and then Khrushchev went and had a good reception." The trip was a huge success and a great diplomatic move, Ghana stayed in the Commonwealth. Elizabeth made the first royal visit to Germany since World War II in 1965—Philip got to return to where he used to live with his sisters, and Elizabeth was cheered in the streets, although that made her uncomfortable, thinking it would remind people too much of a Nazi rally.

Elizabeth was the first to introduce the royal walkabout in Australia and New Zealand, where she wanders among the crowd meeting the locals, because as Elizabeth herself says, "I have to be seen to be believed." She was the first British monarch to visit China, traveling there in 1986. In 1991 on her third state visit to the United States, she was the first British monarch to address both houses of Congress.

In 2002, her Golden Jubilee year marking fifty years on the throne, she takes another royal tour around the Commonwealth, but by her Diamond Jubilee in 2012, she and Philip had started only going on "awaydays," tours in the United Kingdom, sending their children and grandchildren on the overseas tours. Elizabeth once said, "If I wore beige, no one would know who I am." As the world's most traveled monarch, now serving for over 66 years, she probably doesn't need to worry anymore about not being recognized anymore.

GREAT BRITISH ~~~LLY

MR BEAN - A COMEDY C...

It is hard to believe that in just 14 half-hour episodes Rowen Atkinson was able to create a character that has captivated the whole planet, spawned a host of spin-offs and other series, and endured for almost 30 years, but it is true. His strange 'child in a man's body' character (who might even be an alien) captivated millions around the world, and he has become a meme for silly behaviour and petulance. The supporting characters too, especially the long-suffering Teddy and the green mini, are instantly recognizable and are now permanently associated with this bizarre yet ultimately endearing person. His mumbled speech made the physical comedy easy for anyone to understand, without knowing English.

If Mr. Bean has a birthday, it must be the 8th of April 1979, when under the name 'Mr. Box' he appeared in a pilot episode for an ITV show called Canned Laugher. Played by Rowen Atkinson, who also played the other two characters in that show, Mr. Box bears an uncanny resemblance to Mr. Bean, who first debuted under that name in the early 1980s, at the Edinburgh Fringe Festival, a famous trial ground for actors.

Atkinson had begun his life as a choir boy at Durham Cathedral (alongside future Prime Minister Tony Blair), before studying engineering. He had always done humorous impersonations as a boy, to entertain school friends, and acted in school plays, but it was only when he went to Oxford to do an engineering PhD that being an actor started to have serious appeal for him. It was there, in the Oxford University Dramatic Society (OUDS), that he met the comedy writer Richard Curtis. They became life-long friends and colleagues, and Atkinson credits Curtis with encouraging his career. Curtis became co-writer for the Mr. Bean series, along with another friend of Atkinson, the actor and writer Robin Driscoll. Benjamin Elton, another associate of Atkinson from his earlier comedy days, was also a writer for some episodes.

Between 1979 and 1982 Atkinson featured in the satirical show, Not the Nine O'clock News, which parodied the BBC's nightly news broadcast. In 1987 Atkinson appeared at the Just for Laughs comedy festival in Montreal, Canada. In keeping with that country's bilingualism, there was both an English and a French programme. Atkinson asked to appear on the French stage, even though he spoke no French, and the audience was entertained by a character who mumbled rather than spoke. Atkinson wanted to test if his physical comedy was successful in the absence of language, and the incoherent mumbling became an important characteristic of Mr. Bean. It made the show accessible to millions around the world who didn't speak English, and it made the show hugely popular globally.

The first appearance of Mr. Bean was on the 1st of January 1990, as a half-hour special for Thames Television. Further episodes appeared sporadically, between once and four times a year, until the airing of the final episode, number 15, on the 15th of December 1995. He also appeared in five brief sketches between 1991 and 2015 on the charity telethon Comic Relief. He made 15 guest appearances on normally factual TV programs in the UK and around the world, as well as appearing in television commercials.

Who is Mr. Bean? We know little about him, but this strange man is almost always seen in a tweed jacket and thin red tie, often communicating with a brown teddy bear, called Teddy. Often treated as alive, but also used as a tool where it suits Mr. Bean, Teddy acts as a foil for his stunts and an audience for his antics. Mr. Bean lives in a small flat - Flat 2, 12 Arbour Road, in the real north-London area of Highbury. His source of income is mysterious – does he have a trust fund, perhaps, from a rich family, or is he on a disability allowance? After all, it is hard to picture this person

Key Facts

- 14 episodes running from 1990 to 1995
- Featured the bizarre adventures of a man-child in a confusing world
- Starred Rowan Atkinson as Mr. Bean
- Broad international appeal for its physical, not verbal, humour
- Generated spin-off movies and an animated TV series of 134 episodes

holding down a regular job, although we do see him once working as a museum guard, which seems an unlikely occupation, considering his low ability to deal with boredom. Described by Atkinson as 'a child in a man's body', Bean certainly has the curiosity of a child, with very little capacity for normal, adult social interaction, and a 'creative' approach to problem solving. He is also without scruples, cheating on an exam, for example, in the first episode, and often damaging property with impunity.

He is also more than a little paranoid, considering his long-running feud with a tiny three-wheel car, the light-blue 1972 Reliant Regal Supervan III, which appears in many episodes, as a running gag. He cheats too in his own car, a 1977 British Leyland Mini 1000 Mark 4, lime-green with a black hood. He tries to escape paying a parking charge by driving out through the entrance, and the padlock he uses to secure it, as well as once removing the steering wheel, are extreme security measures that also show a perhaps more serious paranoia. He has been variously suggested as suffering from Schizotypal Personality Disorder, Schizoid Personality Disorder, or Autistic Spectrum Disorder. Other aspects of his behaviour, such as his mumbling, have been ascribed to Selective Mutism, but others feel that he is most probably suffering from Generalized Anxiety, of which mumbling can be a symptom, and it is this anxiety that makes him so socially inept and bumbling.

What is almost certain is that it is Mr. Bean's utter inability to do anything in the ordinary way that creates the humour. Thinkers as early as Socrates suggested that a display of self-ignorance invites ridicule, and Aristotle pointed out that we laugh at inferior individuals precisely because we feel pleasure at our own superiority. There is a sense of what Germans called schadenfreude in our laughter at Mr. Bean – his misfortune gives us pleasure. This is often called the Superiority Theory of humour. Children, in particular, enjoy this kind of humour, since they struggle to assert their competence among grown-ups, and someone performing worse than them is sure to be a source of relief through laughter.

If we feel superior to Mr. Bean, we probably feel nothing but sympathy for his 'girlfriend', Irma Gobb (played by Matilda Ziegler), even though we only meet her in three episodes. The classic mismatched couple, Irma is desperate for romance and marriage, but to Mr. Bean, she is just a friend, and someone to act as a foil for his foibles. We become a little uncertain of his true feelings when he becomes jealous of Irma dancing with another man at a disco, and his inability to relate to her romantically could be another symptom of whatever disorders he suffers from. Finally, when he doesn't propose marriage as expected, Irma leaves him and moves on, hopefully to more promising husband material.

An alternative theory for Mr. Bean's strange behaviour is that he is an alien from space. Beginning in episode two he arrives at the beginning of each show in a light beam from the sky, while Southwark Cathedral Choir sings a hymn parody, 'Ecce homo qui est faba' (which translates from Latin as Behold the man who is a bean). At the end of each episode, he beams back up, while the choir sings, Farewell the man who is a bean, in Latin. So is Mr. Bean sent by God, or aliens? The idea that it is aliens is re-enforced in an episode of the animated series, parodying he film Close Encounters of the Third Kind, where he is abducted by aliens who look exactly like him, right down to their teddy bears, before being returned to earth by them in a light beam.

Cultural Impact

Although there were only 15 original episodes, Mr. Bean lived on in several forms. Atkinson made two feature-length films. The first was Bean, released in 1997, set in Los Angeles, and the second was Mr. Bean's Holiday, from 2007, in which he takes a holiday in France, ending up on the French Riviera at the Cannes Film Festival. The films were commercial successes, with each grossing around $250 million globally. Critical reviews were mixed, but it is hard to think seriously about Mr. Bean, in any medium.

He also continued to appear on television, with an animated series running first from 2002 to 2004, with 52 episodes of 22 minutes, and then in a further 78 episodes, starting from 2015. While similar to the original series, with a voice-over by Atkinson, more English is heard mixed with the mumbling, and two new characters, Mr. Bean's landlady, Mrs. Wicket and Scrapper, her vicious, one-eyed cat, are introduced. The arrival of Mrs. Wicket, who Bean is constantly infuriating in one way or another, and who regularly recruits him for household tasks, such as lawn mowing, adds a new dimension to his psychology. She suggests a domineering mother-figure and the possibility that his bumbling and short temper are passive-aggressive retaliation against a controlling mother.

We can get an idea of how deeply Mr. Bean entered the British consciousness, from the fact that he was chosen to appear in the opening of the Summer Olympics held in London in 2012. In the sketch he attempts, as we might expect, to cheat his way to a gold medal.

Atkinson's mime presentation of the character was inspired, he says, by the French mime artist Jacque Tati, and his character Monsieur Hulot. Right from the beginning, he aimed to transcend the limitations of English, and he succeeded. The show enjoys immense popularity globally, and it has been broadcast in almost every country in the world, often with great success, creating a large international fan base. It received a Rose d'Or at the Swiss Light Entertainment Festival in 1991. It was also nominated for several BAFTA awards but never received any. The producer, Peter Bennett-Jones, is quoted as saying in 2015, I don't think anyone could have anticipated quite how successful and long-lived it would be.

Places to Visit

Highbury is a district of London, near Islington, containing a mixture of 18th and 19th century restored villas, terrace housing, and blocks of ex-council flats. A visit gives a good idea of the lives of ordinary Londoners outside the central core of the city.

The grand 1825 façade of the original Arsenal Football Stadium (called Highbury Stadium originally) can be seen at a luxury housing complex called Highbury Square.

At 106 Highbury New Park there is an apartment building called, "The Recording Studio". It was originally Wessex Studios, built by Sir George Martin, the producer of The Beatles, who spent his childhood on Drayton Park, Highbury. Many bands, including the Rolling Stones, Genesis, Queen, the Sex Pistols and the Clash, recorded there.

Where to Watch

- Full sets of all the original episodes, including the two feature films, are available. The A&E Home Video version includes the original opening credits as shown on television, which are not used in other compilations.
- There is a Mr. Bean YouTube channel showing all the episodes in full.
- Netflix and Amazon Prime stream all the episodes and the movies.

Further Research

- Mr. Bean's Diary (1992)
- Mr. Bean's Pocket Diary (1994)
- These two books have identical content, but different formats
- Mr. Bean's Diary (2002)
- A different book, despite the title similarity, released to accompany the animated series
- The Story of Mr. Bean – video documentary
- The Psychology of Humor: An Integrative Approach, by Rod A. Martin & Thomas Ford
- An Introduction to the Psychology of Humor, by Janet M. Gibson

THE FOUNDING OF THE NHS
BRITAIN'S REVOLUTION IN SOCIAL WELFARE

On 5th July 1948, the British Minister for Health, Nye Bevan, strode into Manchester's Davyhulme hospital and declared the new National Health Service open. Britain's National Health Service was a radical innovation, consisting of a state-funded, comprehensive health service that would be free at the point of need and delivery. Based on the principle that no one in Britain should be denied medical care based on economic considerations, this new public service would be a true equalizer in British society: from the poorest to the richest; all would now have access to the same basic treatment.

The NHS was born in the aftermath of the Second World War and represented a significant innovation in public health and planning. Its inception, however, may be dated to early 20th century debates and public concern over public health and welfare, in a period when the extent of poverty across the country demanded a radical solution. The NHS, therefore, represents the culmination of a 50-year revolution in social welfare in British politics and society, creating an enduring legacy that has stood the test of time. The NHS, despite regular and consistent crises of funding, continues to this day as one of the most well-functioning, reliable and cost-effective forms of healthcare in the developed world.

Reimagining Healthcare: Utopian Visions of Post-War Britain

The idea of the National Health Service emerged in political discourse in the immediate aftermath of World War Two, but the idea of social, government-funded healthcare goes back much further. In the late Victorian period, and throughout the early 20th century, there were increasing calls that the burden of caring for the poor should be shifted away from charities and on to the government. The chaos caused by the interwar period, and in particular the Great Depression, had created a huge problem of destitution and poverty that could not be assuaged by private charitable funds, which were uncertain, and instead needed a centralized government approach. In 1919 a commission was set up headed by Lord Dawson, which produced a report that outlined, in theory, the ways in which a nationally run health service might be structured. During the 1920s a gradual transition took place in which the old poor laws were replaced by service-driven local government initiatives. Many of the older charitable institutions were transformed into hospitals for ratepayers, but there was little uniformity, and the quality of service could vary dramatically from region to region. In particular, some regions simply did not have enough specialist services, making effective healthcare a postcode lottery.

These problems were at the centre of political debate, and a number of potential solutions had been circulating for some time in government and policy circles, but it was the Second World War that gave the politicians the impetus they needed to make the change. The Second World War had ushered in a variety of new innovations in healthcare and service provision. The emergency medical service was created to cater to particular needs in the war effort and in response to bombing and bombardment during the Blitz. This showed that it could be possible to create a system that was centrally organized and run, which could function effectively across the country. In addition to this, however, the cataclysmic effect of the war meant that it was much easier to make it possible to completely overhaul the existing system and implement something radical and unprecedented.

Key Dates

- May 1920 - Publication of Lord Dawson's report on medical provision
- November 1942 - Publication of the Beveridge Report
- November 1946 - National Health Service Act is passed in Westminster
- July 1948 - Opening of the NHS across the UK
- June 1952 - Introduction of prescription charges in the NHS

Key Figures

- Sir Bertrand Dawson
  Led a commission into U.K. healthcare provision in 1919
- William Beveridge
  Liberal economist, author of the Beveridge Report
- Winston Churchill
  British Prime Minister (1940-1945; 1951-1955)
- Clement Attlee
  British Prime Minister (1945-1951)
- Aneurin 'Nye' Bevan
  Minister for Health (1945-1951)

The Beveridge Report

During the 1940s, a number of key figures in British politics began to take the idea of a National Health Service seriously. In 1941, during the wartime coalition between the Conservative and Labour parties, a committee was established that would provide a wholesale review of Britain's social insurance and services, in order to assess the country's needs during the war. The ensuing report was drafted by William Beveridge, a liberal economist, who identified five 'Great Evils' in British society that needed to be rooted out as part of any post-war reconstruction effort: ignorance, squalor, idleness, disease and want. In order to tackle these social ills, argued Beveridge, there needed to be a wholesale revolution in social care in the United Kingdom, developing an integrated system that was not stymied by inter-party differences and feuds.

The report said relatively little about the idea of a National Health Service itself, but it did suggest that any system of state welfare needed to have a new health service at its heart. Beveridge believed that an insurance-based system, that would allow individuals to make more than the minimum contribution, would provide the best scheme, but otherwise, his proposals lacked a comprehensive funding plan. Fundamentally, however, the Beveridge Report was a strident call for radical change in the social welfare system and was met by widespread popular approval.

The Conservative leadership, headed by Winston Churchill, whilst acknowledging the need for a post-war plan that addressed the deficit in social welfare, was generally opposed to the idea of the NHS. In particular, the Conservatives were anxious not to create public expectation of a massive influx of public spending on healthcare. However, in 1943, Conservative MP Henry Willink published a white paper calling for the establishment of a National Health Service, funded through central taxation, providing care to anyone who needed it, free at the point of use. Despite strong opposition within the Conservative Party, the ideas stuck, and the election of Clement Attlee's post-war Labour government created the political conditions in which these ideas could become policy.

Attlee's campaign had been run on the idea of the welfare state, with the new health service at the core of his election promises. In the post-war climate, Keynesian economics were back in vogue, and Attlee's promises of high employment, a state welfare system that would follow people from the

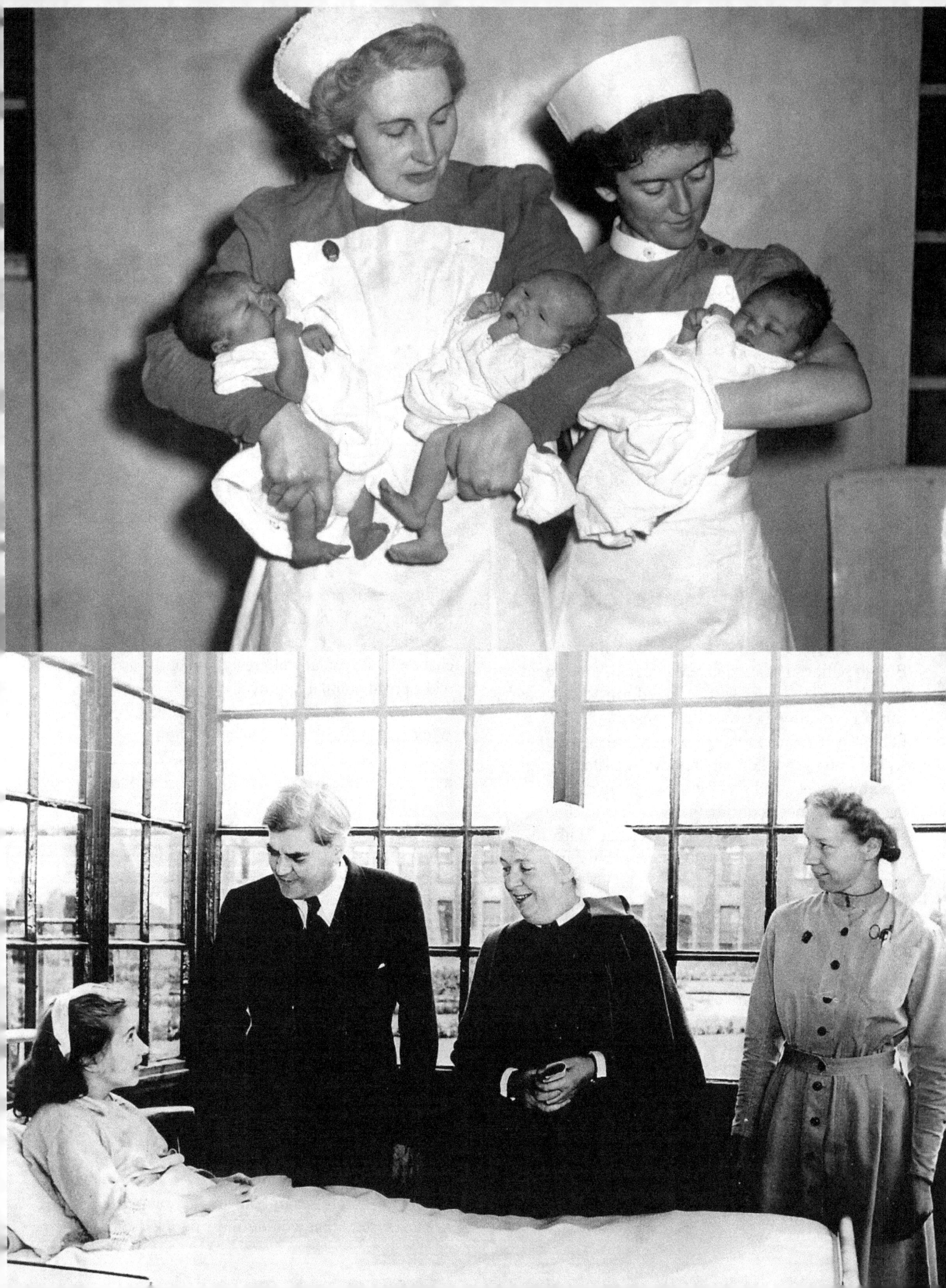

cradle to the grave, and the reconstruction of British society were all attractive propositions to the British electorate. His landslide victory in the general election of 1945 gave him the necessary mandate to implement the new National Health Service. Aneurin 'Nye' Bevan was made Minister for Health and tasked with the challenge of translating the promise of the NHS into a practical reality.

Finding a Format That Worked

Early imagined versions of the health service were divided on how it should be funded and organized. For the Conservatives, the favoured route was one in which local authorities would be empowered to plan and implement health services in their local areas. However, the election victory for Labour in 1945 gave the Labour Party carte blanche to develop a new and revolutionary concept: Bevan proposed a wholly nationalized system that would be regionally run and administered. The principles of the new service were that it should be free at the point of need and that people should have equal access to services and opportunities.

In this regard, the National Health Service in the U.K. was a model unique to the majority of Western democratic systems. Where other states tended to follow an insurance-based model, the British system was completely publicly funded. One of the central and most important tenets of the system was that the health service should be funded through taxation, meaning that if you earned more, you contributed more. Furthermore, the health service would not discriminate between patients. Care would be provided to everyone, on an equal basis, even those who were simply visiting the country.

On the 5th July 1948, the National Health Service was opened, to a widespread positive feeling across the country. The late 1940s were a period of severe austerity, with food rationing still in place, and widespread poverty. Most significantly, there was a fuel shortage and a serious housing crisis. The housing crisis led to significant new demands being placed on the health care system, as new towns were expanding, and there was little money available for building new hospitals. The NHS, therefore, opened in a period of considerable pressure, but nevertheless, it was a welcome boost to British morale, providing a sense of innovation and change that alleviated the post-war malaise.

The new National Health Service was structured according to three principal areas: 1) hospital services, which would be administered by regional boards; 2) primary care, consisting of G.P.s, opticians, pharmacists and dentists, who would work as independent contractors, and 3) community services, consisting of child welfare, maternity services, health visitors and education, and immunization. This tripartite structure formed the basis of the NHS until the 1970s.

Early Successes and Failures

The NHS was, on balance, a profound success, and in addition to achieving its core mission of providing healthcare across the country, it was also a driving force behind a number of scientific and medical advances in the U.K. The NHS was part of a wider boom in healthcare caused by the Second World War. The war had prompted numerous innovations in technology and science, and these extended to healthcare and pharmacology as the pressures of war had fostered new discoveries. In particular, there was a glut of research into mental health, in response to the trauma of war and the effects of advances in psychology. In addition to this, there was also better access to antibiotics, anaesthetics, and other important drugs and medical technologies. The NHS both benefited from and galvanized these developments within the U.K.

Early problems with the new health service emerged as a result of the high expectations set for treatment and availability of services. Provision of services was patchy, and many rural areas did not have access to consultants or specialist services. The expectations of the public were very high as a result of the widespread publicity that surrounded the new scheme, and the costs were not well thought out. The initial costing for the NHS was soon exceeded, and as a result, there was pressure for some services to become individually paid. In 1952 charges were introduced for prescription services and dental treatment. This caused profound problems in the Labour Party leadership, and Nye Bevan, the architect of the NHS, resigned over the outcry.

The NHS has, arguably, been in a state of

financial crisis ever since its inception. As early as 1957, a royal commission was established to conduct an enquiry into NHS spending, and there were public concerns that hospital staff were indulging in wasteful behaviour. Bevan himself addressed this accusation early in the history of the NHS, stating that there would never be sufficient funds to do everything that the NHS hoped to achieve, but that this was not an argument against its existence. Rather, for Bevan, the NHS was an aspirational entity, which could always be improved upon and developed.

Legacy

The foundation of the NHS was an extremely important moment in Britain's post-war history, establishing a principle of social welfare that has endured in the British system to this day. The NHS faces a number of challenges, particularly in recent years where it faces an annual funding crisis generated by seasonal pressures on the service. Nevertheless, the system continues to function well and provides healthcare to millions of patients every year.

In 2017, the healthcare systems of ten developed nations were evaluated against one another, including the USA, Australia, Canada, France, Germany, the Netherlands, New Zealand, Norway, and Switzerland. The U.K.'s NHS was deemed to be the highest-ranking health service overall, scoring higher on metrics such as patient care, affordability and safety. This is despite the fact that the U.K. spends proportionally less on the NHS than other countries do on their healthcare systems. The U.K. spends 9.75% of GDP on the NHS, compared to 17.21% in the USA and 11.27% in Germany. These statistics suggest that despite recent controversies, and the problems of funding that afflict the present-day NHS, the system that developed in a moment of radical post-war change continues to function effectively 70 years later.

Sites to Visit

- Trafford General Hospital in Manchester is generally credited as being the first NHS hospital and is the site where Nye Bevan officially launched the new health service.
- St Bartholomew's Hospital Museum, Smithfield, London. This museum offers a history of medicine in Britain set in one of London's oldest and most prestigious hospitals. The collection contains a wide range of artefacts, artworks, and medical instruments, in addition to the history of the hospital and its transition to a full NHS institution.

Film, Literature and T.V.

- Food for Ravens. BBC drama centred on the life of Nye Bevan, starring Brian Cox (1997).
- The NHS at 60: Stuffing Their Mouths With Gold. Radio play by Jerome Vincent, dramatizing the struggle for a national health service that would be free to all at the point of need.
- Call the Midwife. Television drama following a group of midwives in 1950s Britain. Set in the East End of London, the series showcases the pressures placed upon the NHS in its early years.

Further Research

- Nicklaus Thomas-Symonds, Nye: The Political Life of Aneurin Bevan, (I.B. Tauris, 2014). A comprehensive and readable biography of Nye Bevan, the chief architect of the National Health Service.
- Charles Webster, The National Health Service: A Political History, (Oxford University Press, 1998). This book situates the founding of the NHS in its historical context, focusing on the political forces that shaped its inception and development in the second half of the 20th century.
- Marvin Rintala, Creating the National Health Service: Aneurin Bevan and the Medical Lords, (Frank Cass, 2003). Accessible, detailed and fascinating account of the nature of the founding of the NHS, and the key figures that were instrumental in its conception.

TOP 10 BEAUTIFUL BRITISH LIBRARIES
By John Rabon

Libraries are wonderful places. Well before the internet, they were the one place where all of the world's information was at your fingertips. Both then and now, they still provide not only a great resource for information, but a chance to let imaginations take flight. When it comes to libraries in the United Kingdom, you can find some of the most beautiful centers for fiction and nonfiction in the world.

Bodleian Library

Not surprising that Oxford University would have one of the best libraries in the country. It was established in 1602, which makes it both the main library at the university as well as one of the oldest in the UK. It's also one of only six legal repositories in Britain, which means it can legally ask for a copy of any book published in the United Kingdom. While tours of the library are available, reading anything in the library means you have to become a member by agreeing to its formal declaration. It's actually several libraries spread out across central Oxford. The Radcliffe Camera pictured here is an example of a library and reading room.

Signet Library

The Signet Library belongs to a group of private solicitors known as the Society of Writers to Her Majesty's Signet. The library building was constructed in 1822 with a classical interior designed by Robert Reid and William Stark. King George IV referred to it as "the finest drawing room in Europe, and while this Edinburgh law library still serves the society, it's also used as an event space.

John Rylands Library

Part of the University of Manchester, the John Rylands Library is the sort of place you imagine when you think of a beautiful old library. Built in 1899, it's a Grade I listed structure with stone alcoves, beautiful wooden floors, and red carpets that make it visually stunning. It's also one of the top research libraries in the UK and has a great collection of old texts from a Guttenberg Bible to the Papyrus 52 fragment of the Gospel of St. John.

Library of Birmingham

One of the most modern buildings on this list is also one of the most beautiful. The Library of Birmingham was finished in 2013 and looks like a contemporary layer cake on the outside with stacks that light up at night and an interior that has an equally beautiful book rotunda at its center. The Shakespeare Memorial Room was originally built in 1882 and moved over from the old library, and it holds one of the country's most important collections of the Bard's works.

Liverpool Central Library

Certainly a jewel of the North, the Liverpool Central Library is another gorgeous postmodern design. Also opening in 2013 after a multi-million, the amazing interiors are bolstered by the classical-looking Picton Reading Room, a circular rotunda with a domed roof. Classic and contemporary are a wonderful mix here which are worth checking out.

Duke Humfrey's Library

Found within the Bodleian at Oxford University, Duke Humfrey's Library is the oldest reading room in the library's complex and has sections that date to the 15th, 16th, and 17th Centuries. Like the rest of the Bodleian, it can be seen on the tour of the library's multiple buildings, but actually having reading privileges here will require you to be a member.

Chained Library at Hereford Cathedral

If you remember the library of Kamar-Taj in Marvel's Doctor Strange, the Chained Library at Hereford Cathedral will give you a distinctly similar feel. Books are chained to the library's shelves so they cannot be removed since books were quite valuable in the medieval period. Of course, they're worth quite a lot now as well as the cathedral's collection includes 1,500 older books as well as another 229 medieval manuscripts.

Gladstone's Library

William Gladstone founded this library in Hawarden, Wales out of his personal collection in 1895. The Grade I Victorian building is not only a beautiful reading library with over 150,000 books on history and theology, but it doubles as a bed-and-breakfast. If you want to go to bed with a good book in the natural beauty of the Snowdonia mountains, we can't think of a better place.

Chetham's Library

Also in Manchester, Chetham's Library boasts that it is "the oldest public library in the English-speaking world" and was founded in 1654 as part of Chetham's Hospital. The 17th Century interior is composed of dark wood with gates between the bookshelves that made for perfect reading alcoves. It bears a striking resemblance to the Restricted Section of the Hogwarts Library in Harry Potter, and the adjoining Baronial Hall was almost a filming location before the producers decided on Alnwick Castle.

Sir Duncan Rice Library

Both a university library and a Scottish library, the Sir Duncan Rice Library at the University of Aberdeen has an icy glass exterior that leads you to an equally mesmerizing postmodern interior. This also means that the library boasts wonderful views of the city from each floor, though you'll certainly want to turn your attention to the massive collection which includes books from as far back as the 13th Century.

GREAT BRITISH ICONS
WEDGEWOOD POTTERY

Instantly recognizable, the matt blue pottery with white relief designs of Wedgwood has been as much a part of Britain as the tea poured into the cups since its invention in the 1770s by Josiah Wedgwood. Artist, craftsman, scientist and business innovator, Wedgwood rode the new fashion of Neoclassicism to become a wealthy industrialist. His pieces were in palaces all across Europe, and in the homes of the growing middle-classes too. He developed new methods of production, helping to turn a community of individual craftsmen into a giant industrial complex in Staffordshire. He was also a social activist, working for the abolition of slavery, and creating for that cause a seal that became the first political logo.

The town of Burslem in Staffordshire had been known for its pottery since the 12th century, so it is no surprise to learn that the young Josiah Wedgwood, when only nine years old, was already an accomplished potter. Burslem, along with the five surrounding smaller towns, became the district known as Stoke-on-Trent, the heart of the British potteries. Josiah was born in 1730, and he grew up in a time when the craft of pottery, with its ancient tradition of small, artisan potters working by hand, was being revolutionized and turned into a key industry of the Industrial Revolution. A few years before Josiah was born, there were around 50 artisan potters in Burslem, and several were called Wedgwood – his was an ancient family closely tied to pottery – but all that would change, in large part due to his own efforts.

When he was fourteen, he almost died of smallpox, and the disease left him with a painful and weakened knee. By this point, he was accomplished on the potter's wheel, but his handicap forced him from it, and he turned instead to modelling in clay and design. This was fortuitous because casting pots from models, rather than throwing them on the wheel, was to be the future of industrial pottery.

A key figure in innovating new techniques was Thomas Whieldon, who had established a highly-successful pottery in the area. He was eleven years older than Wedgwood, but on seeing the potential and talent of the younger man, in 1754 he took him into partnership. Wedgwood was just twenty-four. Whieldon was interested in improving manufacturing processes, and Wedgwood had the skills and dedication to tackle issues with glazes, the clays being used, mould-making, and other technical problems. At the time a type of pottery called 'creamware' was popular for domestic use. It was shiny, pale cream in colour, with monochromatic pictures on it. Wedgwood developed and improved the glazes and became the leader in new techniques and methods. In return, Whieldon taught him how to make pottery as an industrial process, instead of as a craft.

Wedgwood's knee problems again put him in the right place, when in 1762, while being treated in Liverpool by a physician, he was introduced to a wealthy country gentleman and businessman, Thomas Bentley. They became friends, and in 1768 entered a partnership to form a new pottery. The site was chosen wisely, straddling the new Trent and Mersey Canal, since lack of transport had been a continuous problem at the more isolated site of Burslem. He was also a backer of the canal, and he built a house on one side, with the factory on the other. He named the site Etruria, and the house, Etruria Hall. Besides the financing provided by his partner Bentley, Wedgwood had made a fortuitous decision to marry his third-cousin, Sarah Wedgwood, in 1764. It was a love-match, against initial opposition from Sarah's father, but she did come with a substantial £4,000 dowry, equivalent to a million dollars today, which became his on their marriage.

In the early 18th century, the dominant artistic style was Rococo, a flamboyant and florid style derived from the earlier Baroque. But across philosophy and the visual arts change was coming. The Age of Enlightenment called for a more refined, intellectual artistic style, and it coincided with the

> **Key Facts**
>
> - Founded by Josiah Wedgwood in 1768
> - 180 years of continuous production at the Etruria factory
> - Created new forms and designs in the Neoclassical fashion
> - Continues production today under foreign ownership

fashion for Grand Tours – a coming-of-age trip around Europe by young men of the upper classes. In Greece and Italy, they saw ruins of ancient empires and brought back antiquities – statues and pottery in particular. Works of Ancient Greece and Rome were copied, and drawings published in books eagerly consumed by intellectual and leaders of fashion. Greek philosophy and idealism came together in a new movement called Neoclassicism.

Josiah Wedgwood was also intrigued by classical works, particularly in ceramics, and he was particularly influenced by pieces collected by Sir William Hamilton, British Ambassador to the Kingdom of Naples. These pieces were assigned to the Etruscans, a pre-Roman civilization in Italy, although in fact many were from ancient Greece. This artwork provided models for Wedgwood to create ceramics with entirely new decorative themes, attuned to the demand for Neoclassical pieces by less affluent followers of the new trend – those unable to own originals.

Just as important as the designs were the techniques and glazes. Two main styles became his trademark works. One was close to an Etruscan original, which he called 'Black Basalt' Ware. This had a mat-black clay body, decorated with ochre figures. The production of this pottery required innovative techniques such as adding manganese to the clay to intensify the depth of colour and firing the pots in the absence of oxygen, which turned the clay black.

Even more famous is his Jasperware. The body of the pots is a distinctive teal-blue colour, decorated with relief figures and patterns in white. The matte finish was a total departure from earlier highly-glazed pottery, and it was particularly well-adapted to austere ornamental pieces suitable for Neoclassical interiors. After 1775 Wedgwood employed John Flaxman to model the relief pieces for some of his work. Flaxman had studied classical sculpture and architecture in Rome, and he became one of the leading figures of British Neoclassicism. Flaxman worked for Wedgwood for 12 years.

Wedgwood was not just innovating with his materials, but in his factory too. He used division of labour to create production lines over a hundred years before Henry Ford would famously do this in his car factories. There was a village for the workers, another innovation that would become more prominent in the 19th century with industrialists such as John Cadbury, of chocolate fame.

Even before Etruria, Wedgwood was successful with his innovations in the more-traditional creamware, receiving orders from nobility, and convincing Queen Charlotte, the wife of King George III, to allow him to call one of his pottery lines 'Queen's Ware'. His stationary announced his royal associations, and this affordable line of pottery was soon being shipped all over the world, thanks to the British fleet of trading ships. He produced a 944-piece dinner service with a frog motif for the Empress Catherine II of Russia. He opened a warehouse and showroom in 1765 on Charles Street, in Mayfair, another in Grosvenor Square, and another on Greek Street called Wedgwood Mews. His display rooms became a fashionable place to be seen, and his Neoclassical designs were all the rage. He had catalogues of his wares printed, employed travelling salesmen, and is credited with inventing many marketing techniques still considered 'modern' today. In the process, he became one of the wealthiest businessmen of the period.

When promoting the Trent and Mersey Canal, Wedgwood had met Erasmus Darwin, and his first daughter, Susannah, married Darwin's son Robert. The couple had a son, Charles, whose work on evolution was made possible by the fortune he inherited from the Wedgwood-Darwin family. Staffordshire became the heart of British manufacturing, supported by global exports to the Empire.

The families were also engaged with the social and political issues of the day. In 1787 the Society for the Abolition of the Slave Trade was founded, and Josiah was on the organizing committee. Sarah Wedgwood was also involved in the campaign. They used the mail to promote the cause, and they wanted a stamp to use on the sealing-wax with which letters were sealed at that time. Josiah had one of his designers create the stamp, which showed a kneeling African in chains, with the words, Am I Not a Man and a Brother? above the figure. The design became a campaign hit, and it was reproduced on everything from cufflinks to snuff boxes, and on printed literature too. It is often considered to be the first major use of a logo for a political cause.

In 1790 Wedgwood formed a partnership with two of his sons and a nephew, becoming

Wedgewood & Sons. The sons left a few years later, but the firm continued as a family business. In 1795 Josiah died, but the business, and innovation, continued under his son Josiah II. In response to the taste among the upper-classes for imported Chinese porcelain tea services, they began to manufacture bone-china, which became a less-expensive substitute for the imported products. The strength of Wedgwood continued to be its upper-class cachet at middle-class prices, creating aspiration products for those climbing out of the working-class. But tastes changed, and the Queen's tableware gradually changed into your mother's tableware.

The Etruria works continued in production for 180 years, closing only in the 1940s. Subsidence from mining underneath the factory led to the construction of a new factory a short distance away, at Barlaston. In 1968 Wedgwood bought up several rival companies, consolidating its grip on the industry. In 1979 they purchased an American company, Franciscan Ceramics, but a few years later the Los Angeles factory was closed, and production of the brand was moved to Staffordshire. Then in 1986, the company was purchased by Waterford Glass, an Irish crystal glass company of a similar age, and with a similar historical trajectory. Although Wedgwood itself continued to be profitable, the Waterford Wedgwood Group was never financially strong. The 2008 financial crisis put the company into receivership, and after lay-offs and closures, it was bought by Fiskar, a Finnish company, in 2015. The Wedgwood label is still being made at Barlaston.

Sites to Visit

- Josiah Wedgwood's grave is in St Peter ad Vincula Churchyard, Glebe Street, Stoke-on-Trent, Staffordshire.
- The town of Burslem, part of the city of Stoke-on-Trent, is today one of the last remaining places where the tradition of living among the factories you work in continues. Sections of the canals that pass through the old pottery areas are rich in the industrial heritage of Britain. A trip provides a real insight into life outside the south-east of England and a view of an altogether different country. Sadly, the award-winning Ceramica museum in the town was closed due to lack of funds.
- Etruria Hall, designed by Joseph Pickford, is today the meeting and events centre of the Stoke on Trent Moat House Hotel, part of the Best Western chain.
- The Wedgwood Museum, Barlaston, Stoke-on-Trent, is adjacent to the factory. It dates from 1906 and moved from Etruria with the factory. The collections are formally owned by the Victoria & Albert Museum, on permanent loan back to Wedgwood. It is open every day from 10 am to 5 pm.
- The World of Wedgwood is located near the Museum. It is an interactive display and can be linked to tours of the factory. There is a train station servicing the location.
- All that remains of the Etruria Works is a round tower, called the Round House, on Etruria Road, Stoke-on-Trent.
- There is blue plaque at 12, Greek Street, London W1, marking the location of the Wedgwood Mews display rooms.

Further Research

- Wedgwood: A Story of Creation and Innovation, by Gaye Blake-Roberts and Alice Rawsthorn, 2017
- Wedgwood: The First Tycoon, by Brian Dolan, 2004
- Wedgewood By Rathbone: Reprint in Its Entirety with an Added Index of Old Wedgewood, by Frederick Rathbone, 1968 (published by the Wedgwood Museum)

GREAT BRITONS
The Writer Lady Mary Wortley Montagu

Letter writing was a major occupation of the wealthy classes in the 18th and 19th centuries. Few wrote as many as Lady Mary Wortley Montagu, who described in detail her travels and insights on life in the Ottoman Empire. The beautiful daughter of a member of the Court of Charles I, she was disfigured by smallpox. Later she pioneered inoculation with live smallpox as a protection, having both of her children inoculated, and introducing the practice to the Court. By affecting Turkish dress and disseminating information of life in the Ottoman Empire, especially that of women, she contributed to the later Orientalism fashion in Europe. She spent the latter part of her life living in Italy. Her letters were published posthumously. Her son Edward went on to be a notable traveler and eccentric, also affecting Turkish dress, and converting to Islam.

Instead of travel forum posts, tweets and selfies, travellers of the past – and indeed everyone literate – wrote letters. Long, extensive and frequent letters. If you were rich, you most probably spent every morning, after your toilette and breakfast, doing your 'correspondence' for several hours. Carefully hand-written letters passed back and forth between family members, friends and professional colleagues, and contained factual information as well as personal opinions and news. So important was letter writing that the first novels were written as a fictitious exchange of letters, most famously perhaps in Tobias Smollett's, The Expedition of Humphry Clinker. This book is generally considered one of the finest early English novels. It was published in 1771, and it takes the form of correspondence of a trip around England.

This was surely a novel that would have appealed to Lady Mary Wortley Montagu – had she not died nine years earlier. Lady Montagu was a prolific letter writer, and she is remembered mostly for her letters written while travelling in the Ottoman Empire, a significant accomplishment at such an early time.

Lady Mary was born into a position of prestige. He father was Evelyn Pierrepont, 1st Duke of Kingston-upon-Hull. He had risen from the position of a lowly MP through the peerage to become a Duke in 1715 and was the Lord President of the Council, one of the most powerful positions in the country, and head of the King's Privy Council. Mary had been born in May 1689, when her father was still an MP, and grew up as her family ascended the social and political ladder.

Key Facts

- Born 1689 – died 1762
- Prolific letter writer of her travels and opinions
- Early promoter of smallpox inoculation
- Increased knowledge and interest in the lives of Ottoman women

At the tender age of seven, she came to the attention of the Kit-Kat Club. This was a society of prominent literary and political figures who met at the Fountain Tavern on The Strand, among other venues. The main activity of the members was the toasting of beautiful women, in glasses especially engraved with those women's names. These were often wives or mistresses of members, so the addition of Lady Mary at such a young age is suggestive of her great beauty. Highly intelligent too, she chafed under the restrictions of a girl's limited home education, and she taught herself Latin from her father's libraries. By 14 she had already written two albums of poetry, a brief novel, and a prose-and-verse romantic play.

When twenty Mary was being courted by two men - Edward Wortley Montagu and Clotworthy Skeffington. Her father favoured Skeffington, who was going to inherit an Irish peerage. He rejected Montagu because he refused to entail his estate – that is, ensure it would only go to a male heir. Mary, however, would have none of this, and chose to scandalously elope with Edward Montagu, grandson of Edward Montagu, 1st Earl of Sandwich, a lawyer at the Inner Temple, and clearly a much more effective letter writer. (Courtship in those circles was mainly conducted by correspondence). The couple were married in August 1712, and in May of the following year a son was born, also called Edward. Her joy must have been shattered by the death from smallpox of her brother just a few weeks later.

In 1714 Edward was made Junior Commissioner

On Smallpox

> I am going to tell you a thing, that will make you wish yourself here. The small-pox, so fatal, and so general amongst us, is here entirely harmless.... There is a set of old women, who make it their business to perform the operation, every autumn, in the month of September, when the great heat is abated. People send to one another to know if any of their family has a mind to have the small-pox; they make parties for this purpose, and when they are met (commonly fifteen or sixteen together) the old woman comes with a nut-shell full of the matter of the best sort of small-pox, and asks what vein you please to have opened. She immediately rips open that you offer her, with a large needle (which gives you no more pain than a common scratch) and puts into the vein as much matter as can lie upon the head of her needle, and after that, binds up the little wound with a hollow bit of shell...

of Treasury, and the family moved from the country to London, becoming members of the Court of Charles I. Mary soon became a prominent figure at the Court, but at the end of 1715, she too contracted smallpox. Although she survived, her beauty was permanently damaged by the disfiguring scars which this terrible disease invariably left in its wake. Voltaire wrote that at the time, 60% of the population would catch smallpox, and only 20%, or one in three of those infected, would survive it.

In 1716, Edward was appointed Ambassador to the Ottoman Empire, and they travelled, via Austria, to Istanbul, remaining there until the end of 1718. They had a daughter while there, called Mary. Lady Mary corresponded extensively while travelling, and while living in Istanbul. Her letters were later edited by her and eventually published as The Turkish Embassy Letters. As a woman, she had special access to women's living quarters and their lives, and her letters provide a unique insight into the customs and practises of Moslem women of that time. She tended to take a position that in many ways, their lives were superior to that of women in Europe. Her letters in their original forms were read by many influential friends back home. Lady Mary is depicted in several portraits dressed in Turkish dress, and her influence may have contributed to the latter wave of Orientalism that would become very fashionable in art, decorating and costume in the late 18th and early 19th centuries.

While in Turkey, Lady Mary encountered the practice of inoculation for smallpox, or variolation as it was called. This was widespread among the Turks, who are said to have learned it in turn from the Circassians, an Islamic people who lived near present-day Georgia. Mary saw that they took pus from a person infected with a mild case of smallpox and placed it on a scratch in the arm of another person, giving them a mild infection, which protected them from further infection. The procedure was risky since it used live smallpox. The person inoculated still had a risk of dying, although that was slight compared to the risk from a full infection. Variolation had been reported to Europe a few years earlier, in letters to the Royal Society of London, but it had received little publicity. Lady Mary was to change all that.

Because of her own damaged looks, she wanted to protect her children. In March 1718 she had the embassy surgeon, Charles Maitland, inoculate her 5-year-old son, Edward. She described the procedure extensively and enthusiastically in letters to friends. Back in London, she had Maitland inoculate her daughter, in the presence of the Court physicians. Interest spread among members of the Court. In 1721 Maitland was given permission for a trial on six inmates of Newgate prison, observed by Royal Society members. All the prisoners survived, and Maitland would go on to inoculate the two children of the Prince of Wales the following year. This led to widespread acceptance of variolation. It would be the end of the century before Edward Jenner would develop the vaccination process, using cowpox, that overcame the problems of vaccination and ultimately eradicated the dreaded disease.

In England, Lady Mary continued the life of an aristocrat, raising her children, editing her letters and corresponding. She had a one-way romance with the poet Alexander Pope, who she rejected, much to his humiliation and later anger. He children were difficult. Her daughter copied her mother and eloped with the 3rd Earl of Bute, against the wishes of her mother. Edward ran away regularly as a boy and had to be placed with a strict tutor and send travelling around the world. He spent time in the military and even served as an MP, but he resumed travelling and became a well-known eccentric, converting first to Catholicism and then to Islam, wearing Turkish dress and affecting Turkish manners. His mother left him one guinea in her will.

In 1736 Lady Mary began a full-blown affair with Francesco Algarotti, an Italian man of letters and an art collector. When he left England, she followed him to Venice in 1739, pretending to be taking a winter break in the south of France for her health. For the next two decades, she travelled throughout Italy, staying in all the major cities, as well as spending four years in Avignon, France. During all this time she continued to correspond with friends and family, especially her daughter, who she had forgiven for her elopement.

In 1762, while living in Venice, she received news of her husband's death and returned to London. On route, she left her Turkish Embassy Letters with a certain Reverend Benjamin Sowden of Rotterdam, for safe-keeping, and to be dispos'd of as he thinks proper. After her return to England, she died, just a few months later, on the 21st of August 1762.

Sites to Visit

- Simpson's-in-the-Strand Restaurant, 100 Strand, London WC2, stand on the site of the Fountain Tavern, a haunt of the Kit-Kat Club.
- Wortley Hall, the residence of Lady Mary and later of her daughter, is in the South Yorkshire village of Wortley, south of Barnsley. It is today used as a meetings venue and for weddings. The extensive grounds are open to visitors.

Further Research

- The complete letters of Lady Mary Wortley Montagu, 3 volumes, ed. Robert Halsband, 1965-67
- The Turkish Embassy Letters, ed. Teresa Heffernan & Daniel O'Quinn, 2012
- Letters of Lady Mary Wortley Montague: Written During Her Travels in Europe, Asia, and Africa, to Which Are Added Poems by the Same Author, by Lady Mary Wortley Montagu, 2017
- Lady Mary Wortley Montagu: Comet of the Enlightenment, by Isobel Grundy, 2001
- Lady Mary Wortley Montagu and the Eighteenth-Century Familiar Letter, by Cynthia Lowenthal, 1994
- The Toast of the Kit-Cat Club: A life of Lady Mary Wortley Montagu, by Linda France, 2005

THE ORIGINAL FASHION STREET
London's Savile Row
By Laura Porter

There is a street in Mayfair that is synonymous with traditional men's bespoke tailoring. From the Restoration (1660) to the start of World War Two (1939), British style dominated men's clothing. The British Empire put bespoke-clad men in charge of a quarter of the world's population. Italian tailors copied the styles worn by the Row-clad men on their Grand Tour adapting to make it more suitable to the heat of southern Italy.

Bespoke tailoring means a suit is cut and made by hand. An individual paper pattern is made for each customer and refined over several fittings to achieve a superior fit that surpasses ready-to-wear or made-to-measure. In terms of style, Savile Row suits tend to be sharper, use more shoulder padding and canvas, and prioritise straight, angular lines.

HISTORY

Built in 1674, there was "a fine House and Ground" on the site of 1 Savile Row that was demolished in 1730 when Savile Street, as it was originally known, was planned. Houses were initially only on the east side, but in the 19th century, houses were built on the west side. This explains why the house numbers are consecutive on the east side, whereas it is usually odd numbers on one side and evens on the opposite.

Part of the Burlington Estate, Savile Street was built between 1731 and 1735. Henry Flitcroft was the street's main architect, although no.1 and 22–23 Savile Row were designed by William Kent.

The 3rd Earl of Burlington was known as the 'Architect Earl' as he was the principal patron of the Palladian movement in England. He paid for William Kent to publish Henry Flitcroft drawings in 'The Designs of Inigo Jones' in 1727. His wife was Lady Dorothy Savile and is who the street is named after.

The first residents of Savile Street were mainly military officers and their wives. Politicians moved in, including William Pitt the Younger. And Irish-born dramatist, owner of London Theatre Royal Drury Lane and MP, Richard Brinsley Sheridan lived at 14 Savile Row in 1813–16, till his death.

Phileas Fogg, the hero of Jules Verne's 1873 novel 'Around the World in Eighty Days', is noted in the book's first line as living at "No. 7 Saville Row, Burlington Gardens, the house in which Sheridan died in 1814".

It became a street of doctor's surgeries then, by the late 18th century, tailors moved into the area to be near to affluent customers. In 1846, Henry Poole, credited as the creator of the dinner jacket or tuxedo, opened an entrance at 37 Savile Row from his late father's tailoring premises at 4 Old Burlington Street. Glass frontages were added to the houses for more natural light, so the original Burlingtonian design has been mostly lost, though no.14 still retains much of the original external features.

Savile Row was extended to Conduit Street in 1937–38, but the men's tailors have preferred the original houses.

I went to visit some of the tailors as part of the annual Open House London weekend that takes place each September. Let me share some of the highlights of this famous street.

1 Savile Row

Gieves and Hawkes is one of the oldest continual bespoke tailoring companies in the world. Thomas Hawkes set up his first shop in 1771 in Brewer Street selling to commanders of the British Army, through which King George III became a customer. He moved to no.17 (later number no.14) Piccadilly in 1793, where he gained the first of many Royal Warrants in 1809. James Watson Gieve was a Royal Navy tailor in Portsmouth. He formed a partnership with Joseph Galt in 1852 and bought the remaining shares to form Gieves & Co a year before he died in 1888.

Built in 1732, no.1 Savile Row was the townhouse of the Fairfax family. In 1871, ownership passed to the Royal Geographical Society. On 23 December 1912, Hawkes & Co. bought no.1 Savile Row

Photos - Clockwise from Left: Norton and Sons Tailor Dummy, Gieves and Hawkes Facade, Gieves and Hawkes Interior, Gieves and Hawkes archive

from the RGS for £38,000. It wasn't until 1974 that Gieves Ltd acquired Hawkes & Co. and the company was renamed Gieves & Hawkes.

I got to see the archives where the oldest uniform is a Cheshire Militia uniform from about 1830. A real highlight was the display of the current uniforms of The Honorable Corps of Gentlemen at Arms, the Sovereign's personal bodyguard, consisting of 5 officers and 25 gentlemen. The Corps date back to the time of Henry VIII and Hawkes & Co has been supplying individual officers since the second half of the 19th century. Today, the officers and gentlemen of The Royal Bodyguard attend Her Majesty up to twelve times a year. They are robed and accoutred at no.1 Savile Row before leaving for State Occasions at Buckingham Palace, Windsor Castle or The Houses of Parliament.

There were customer ledgers on display with royalty including Prince Leopold (Queen Victoria's uncle),
Prince Albert (Queen Victoria's Consort), Queen Victoria, Edward VII and our current Queen. A uniform on display was made for Viscount Althorp, later 7th Earl Spencer, the paternal grandfather of Diana Princess of Wales and maternal great grandfather of Princes William and Harry.

It's a stunning corner building with a first-floor balcony level and beautiful ironwork. The ceiling cornices and architectural mouldings in each room remind you of the building's heritage.

3 Savile Row

Built-in 1735, the building was once bought by Lord Nelson for his mistress Lady Hamilton. But this Grade II* listed terraced townhouse is most well-known as the home of the Beatles' multimedia corporation Apple Corps from July 1968. The rooftop was the site of the band's last public performance on 30 January 1969.

The building remained under Apple ownership until 1976. In 2013, US clothes brand Abercrombie & Fitch opened here to protests from the street's tailors. The street is now designated a "special policy area" to make it harder for developers and landlords to dilute the area's distinctive character by allowing chain stores to force out smaller independent businesses.

10 Savile Row

Founded in 1865, Dege & Skinner is one of the oldest bespoke tailoring companies to be in continuous operation in the world. It is also one of only two left on Savile Row to still be a family-run business (the other being Henry Poole & Co).

Most famous for its military tailoring, the tailoring house has obtained three Royal Warrants, one for HM Queen Elizabeth II (1984), one for HM The Sultan Of Oman (1981) and one for HM The King Of Bahrain (2003). Further illustrious clients have included military jackets for Michael Jackson as well as the concierge and doorman uniforms for the staff of Trump Tower. It is also the only house on the Row to have its own shirt cutting facility on site.

Dege & Skinner is known for its innovation with suiting – its most famous design being the unique "Phitwell" shooting jacket which has lacing in the back to help the coat move while holding your gun. An umbrella is used as a firearm substitute during fittings, but one client preferred to use the real thing, so a shotgun is kept in a fitting room (its barrels are blocked and firing pins removed).

11 Savile Row

Huntsman was established in 1849 but only moved to no.11 Savile Row a century later in 1919. This Grade II* listed traditional Georgian terraced house has a Blue Plaque for physician Richard Bright (1789–1858) and the building has also been an asylum (mental institution) which is where stories of ghosts originate from.

Huntsman's equestrian tailor heritage can still be seen on one of the fitting rooms where a leather saddle is mounted for riding breeches fittings. And the stag heads on the walls were shooting trophies

Photos - Top: Norton and Sons workroom, Bottom Left: Norton and Sons Royal Hassar jacket, Bottom Right: Gieves and Hawkes headwear

left by a customer who never returned. Today, they offer exclusive tweeds for the modern tailored wardrobe woven at one of the world's oldest mills, on the Isle of Islay in Scotland.

12, 12a and 13 Savile Row

This pair of terrace houses are Grade II listed. No.12 has stone obelisks in front of the doorway. The entrance door is from the 19th century with a semi-circular fanlight. It is now home to Chittleborough & Morgan who were the leading proponent of the Tommy Nutter style on Savile Row. (Joe Morgan and Roy Chittleborough worked with Nutter as cutters.)

No.12a has a plaque commemorating the residence of historian George Grote (1794–1891).

Richard Anderson is on the ground floor of no.13 Savile Row which has mid-19th century cast iron balconettes to the first floor where you will find Cad & The Dandy.

Richard trained at Huntsman, rising to be head cutter before leaving to set up his own establishment. The house style has its origins in the traditional hacking coat, but the company also offers a line of house denim, and raincoats especially made to fit over his bespoke suits.

On the first floor, Cad & The Dandy opened on Savile Row in 2013 founded by two bankers made redundant in the 2008 recession. While neither had tailoring experience, they have grown the company by providing an affordable bespoke service and a 'semi-bespoke' (a half hand-stitched, half machine-made alternative) from under £1,000.

15 Savile Row

As noted earlier, Henry Poole & Co. is credited as the creator of the dinner jacket. Poole made a short evening jacket for the Prince of Wales (future Edward VII) in 1860 that was admired by James Potter, an American businessman who spent a weekend at Sandringham. Potter had a jacket made and wore it at the Tuxedo Club in New York, which started a trend. As a result, the dinner jacket became known as a tuxedo or tux in America.

Being the first tailors to move into the street, Henry Poole is steeped in tradition. The walls are covered in warrants from royalty all over the world, and its workshops downstairs extend beneath two different buildings. Poole's style is of the traditional, military variety but without the more extreme lines of Huntsman. There also tends to be less padding in the shoulder.

I was told there is a secret doorway on Heddon Street that links to this building so customers not wishing to attract attention can leave discreetly.

16 Savile Row

One of the basements Henry Poole & Co. spreads into is at no.16 Savile Row. On the ground floor of this Grade II listed building is Norton and Sons which was once the home of Sir Benjamin Collins Brodie, who was physician to George IV, William IV and Queen Victoria.

Founded by Walter Charles Norton on the Strand in 1821, Norton & Sons originally pitched itself as a tailor for men who worked in the City. They moved to Conduit Street in the 1850s and arrived at no.16 Savile Row in the 1860s.

In 1970, the label was sold to the Hardy Amies-trained tailor John Grainger and later bought by Patrick Grant in 2005. This enviably handsome man did not train as a tailor, but his savvy business sense and impeccable personal style have seen him featured on TV programmes such as the BBC's The Great British Sewing Bee.

This relatively small store only uses British made cloths. One suit is made by five people and costs from £4,400 to £25,000. They produce just 150 to 200 suits a year but say a good suit will last you a lifetime. They have dressed international royalty, three US Presidents, Winston Churchill, Cary Grant, and Anthony J Drexel Biddle – the first man to be named America's Best Dressed Man.

The shop area has a crocodile-type dinosaur fossil that is millions of years old on display plus an

1800's Royal Hussar's jacket with a 28-inch waist and 32-inch chest.

17 Savile Row

No. 17 was the residence of the architect George Basevi (1832–42), a pupil of Sir John Soane. His designs included Belgrave Square in London and the Fitzwilliam Museum in Cambridge.

This Grade II listed terraced house has some interesting exterior features including wrought iron railings and original stone obelisks in front of the doorway with snuffers (which can also be seen at no.12a). In the days before street lighting, a 'Link Boy' was employed to carry a flaming torch to lead your way after dark. When you reached your destination, the iron horn-shaped snuffer was used to extinguish the flame.

There are more tailors and more houses along Savile Row, but I hope this gives you an insight into the British home of men's tailoring.

THE VULCAN BOMBER
Britain's Cold War Detterent

Avro Aircraft was created during the first years of flight, by Alliot Verdon Roe. The company grew during WWI, but declined during peace, and was sold by Roe to Armstrong Siddeley, keeping its own name. Seeking a plane to carry Britain's nuclear bombs, Avro designers were inspired by the work of German airplane designer Alexander Lippisch to create a delta-wing aircraft capable of flying close to the speed of sound. The Vulcan, named after the Roman god of fire and destruction, became the key element in Britain's nuclear deterrent during the Cold War, sitting armed and ready to fly at every Royal Air Force field. In 1982 it flew missions in the Falklands War, using in-air refuelling to cover the distances. The plane was withdrawn from active service in 1984.

Extended adolescence is a modern invention, so no eyebrows would have been raised when Alliott Verdon Roe, a doctor's son from Eccles, Lancashire, headed out for British Columbia when he was fourteen. He was drawn by a silver-rush to work as a surveyor, but when he arrived the rush was over, and he spent a year kicking around, before returning to England. Back home he apprenticed with the Lancashire & Yorkshire Railway and then failed in an attempt to join the Royal Navy. Instead, he joined the Merchant Navy as an engineer, and while passing those long days at sea, he became fascinated – like many mariners before him – with the effortless flight of the albatross.

Determined to develop a flying machine – the Wright brothers had just made their first flight – he talked his way into the job of Secretary of the newly-formed Aero Club of Great Britain. He quickly moved on to a job as a draughtsman for G.L.O. Davidson, an early airplane maker. He began making model planes, and when he won £75 from the Daily Mail newspaper for one of his designs, the money went towards building the full-sized version, the Roe I Biplane. This first flew successfully in 1908, with an engine he borrowed from France, at the historic Brooklands aerodrome. He moved his experiments to Walthamstow Marshes, an area of common land in Hackney, London, and in July 1909 he made the first all-British flight with a triplane version of his design, dubbed the Avroplane.

Alliot and his brother Humphrey returned to Manchester, and in January 1910 formed the A.V. Roe Aircraft Co. soon to become Avro Aircraft. The company was successful, selling over 8,000

Key Facts

- First British delta-wing aircraft
- Key component of British nuclear deterrent in the Cold War
- Used as a conventional bomber in the Falklands War
- Created by Avro Aircraft, founded by Alliot Verdon Roe

Avro 54 Biplanes to the Royal Airforce They were widely used in WWI. But with peace came financial problems and two-thirds of the company was acquired by a car manufacturer who needed the factory space. Avro moved out to the Cheshire countryside, but in 1928 the car company, Crossley Motors, sold it to Armstrong Siddeley Holdings Ltd. Roe cashed out, sold his shares in Avro, and moved on to a new company – Saunders-Roe – on the Isle of Wight. In 1929 he was knighted for his achievements.

Avro made training biplanes for the Royal Air Force, and as tensions grew during the 1930s, they returned to combat aircraft. Their best-known plane of WWII is the Lancaster Bomber, of which over 7,000 were built, many at a 1.5 million square foot factory camouflaged with a roof of fields and hedgerows. The years following the war were not a period of de-militarization. On the contrary, nuclear weapons and the confrontation between Russia and the West created many opportunities for arms manufacturers, and Avro continued to work with the Air Force. In October 1952, at the remote Montebello Islands, of the north-west coast of Australia, Britain became the world's third nuclear power, exploding a 25-kiloton plutonium bomb in a shallow lagoon. But how was Britain to deliver its new nuclear deterrent?

This had in fact not been overlooked, and as early as 1947, while the nuclear bomb was still under development, the Air Force had tended for "a medium-range bomber landplane capable of carrying one 10,000 lb bomb to target 1,500 nautical miles from a base which may be anywhere in the world." Avro was one of six companies who took up the tender, and once the design team, led by technical director Roy Chadwick and chief designer Stuart Davies. got to work, they quickly saw that a conventional aircraft could not satisfy the specification. The plane also had to be capable of cruising at 580 mph between 35,000 ft and 50,000 ft, and Avro knew little about high-speed flight.

The inspiration came from German research of WWII into swept-wing and delta-wing aircraft. Much of this had been done by the German airplane designer Alexander Lippisch, who had built a series of delta-wing aircraft in the 1930s. Lippisch was one of the German scientists taken to America when the war ended, and he was to design the first American delta-wing jets, particularly the F-102 Delta Dagger interceptor fighter and the B-58 Hustler, the first Mach 2 nuclear bomber. Avro seems to have developed the delta-wing independently, without contact with Lippisch, from the basic swept-wing idea. Starting from that basic concept of sloping the leading edge of the wing by 45o, they then removed the tail and rear fuselage, gaining stability with vertical stabilizer fins on the wingtips. These were later replaced with a central fin along the top of the fuselage. The plane was to be powered by turbo-jet engines.

Numerous trials and tests were needed, and the Avro 707 and 710 were created to test the delta-wing design. A test pilot died in one failed test. Roy Chadwick was also killed in the crash of another Avro plane, but progress was being made. Wind-tunnel tests led to further modifications of the wing design, and on August 30, 1952, the first prototype of the bomber, the VX770, flew for the first time.

In September 1952 all three planes were seen by the public at the Farnborough Air Show. They were quickly nicknamed 'Tin Triangles'. A name was indeed needed for the plane, and after numerous suggestions from the company and the airplane media, the supreme body of the Air Force, the Air Council, chose Vulcan, the Roman god of metalwork, but also of fire and destruction. The aircraft entered into preliminary production, and after further modifications, it received the necessary Certificate of Airworthiness in April 1956, after final testing by the Aeroplane and Armament Experimental Establishment (A&AEE) at Boscombe Down.

These years after the war were the beginning of Britain's long decline. Although the economy grew, it lagged behind the US and was being overtaken by the more rapid recovery of Europe from the devastation of war. The Empire was crumbling and had lost the jewel in its Crown when it was forced in 1947 to grant Indian independence. Malaya became embroiled in a 12-year guerrilla war, starting in 1948. The Mau Mau Rebellion in Kenya started in 1952. The Middle East was in turmoil, and the events leading to the Suez Crisis of November 1956 were already in motion. England wanted to show that it was still a player on the world stage, and becoming a nuclear power was seen as the way to achieve that. The 'special relationship' with the USA was vital to both sides in confronting the Soviet Union. The Vulcan Bomber was the lynch-pin that held it all together.

So when in September 1956 the Air Force received the first Vulcan B.1, the XA897, it was sent around the world, to be displayed in the distant parts of the Empire and in the countries of the Commonwealth. The new Queen, Elizabeth II wanted the Commonwealth to be how Britain would continue to express its supremacy, and the display of new technology and lethal power was the method chosen. The tour was a great success, but when the plane landed back at Heathrow Airport a month later, it crashed due to weather conditions. The pilot and co-pilot ejected and survived, but four passengers were killed, and the plane was completely destroyed. One or two Vulcans were to crash in almost every year it was in service.

In 1959 in-air refuelling was developed for the Vulcan, giving it a longer strategic range. The first nuclear bomb it carried was the low-yield fission bomb, Blue Danube. After the US developed the hydrogen bomb, Britain used variations of US bombs, before developing its own, Yellow Sun. Later a missile bomb, Blue Steel, became the standard weapon fitted. After 1962 there were two fully-armed Vulcans, at 15-minutes' readiness, at every RAF base, with Soviet targets. When Britain made the Polaris submarine its major nuclear deterrent, the Vulcan became less central, but still continued to be kept armed and ready.

The only combat use of the Vulcan was in the 1982 Falklands War, carrying a conventional bomb load. In-air refuelling was used to allow them to reach this distant target, and they took part in several bombing raids. One plane had to make an emergency landing in Brazil, after dumping its

Vulcan in formation with the RAF Red Arrows

missiles and secret documents, where the plane and pilot were held until the war ended. The Vulcan was withdrawn from active service in 1984, and a display unit was maintained for air-shows and fly-overs until 1993.

Sites to Visit

Vulcan bombers can be seen at:

- The Imperial War Museum, Duxford, Cambridgeshire
- The Royal Air Force Museum, Colindale, London
- Southend Airport, Essex
- Woodford Aerodrome, Manchester
- The last flight-worthy Vulcan, XH558, made its last flight in September 2015. It was at the National Aviation Academy, Doncaster, and it will be moved at some point in the future to a display hanger at the Doncaster Sheffield Airport.

Further Research

- Vulcan Boys: From the Cold War to the Falklands: True Tales of the Iconic Delta V Bomber, by Tony Blackman
- AVRO VULCAN Manual 1952 onwards (B2 model): An insight into owning, restoring, servicing and flying Britain's legacy Cold War bomber (Owners' Workshop Manual), by Tony Blackman and Alfred Price
- Vulcan Units of the Cold War, by Andrew Brookes and Chris Davey
- Vulcan: Last of the V-Bombers, by Duncan Cubitt and Ken Ellis
- Vulcan: God of Fire (Video) Directed by Philip Osborn

THE SLANG PAGE
British Home Improvement Words and Phrases by John Rabon

Between the United States and the United Kingdom, the words and phrases we used to describe everyday things can change. Even though we're both speaking English, etymology can vary widely, and the same item or activity might leave you scratching your head when you hear it coming from someone on the other side of the pond. This extends even to home improvement, which is colloquially known in Britain as "Do It Yourself" or "DIY". So if you find yourself in a DIY store looking to fix up the plumbing or something else gone wrong in your house or flat, better learn these terms so you'll know what to get.

Bodge Job

A "bodge job" is typically one that's gone quite wrong. If you hired a handyman whose workmanship wasn't good enough because it was done cheaply or in a hurry, it could break again, which would make it a bodge job.

Stanley Knife

In America, we would typically call this a box cutter or a utility knife. Much like Kleenex, Band-Aid, or Post-It, this tool in Britain has become a generic trademark, or a brand name that has become so synonymous with the item itself that all similar products are referred to by the trademark name.

Wire Wool

This one seems so straight forward you might wonder why we don't call it the same thing. Wire wool for Brits is what Americans call steel wool. Both names are rather apt as this material is made from steel wires bundled very finely so that they form an abrasive surface that's good for finishing work.

Silicone Sealant

This name is a little more upfront in Britain than in America, where we typically call it caulk. While caulk is made from silicone, the origins of the term go back to the 14th Century where it began use as a verb meaning "to stop up cracks and crevices". "Caulking" came into being in the 18th Century, though calling silicone sealant "caulking material" started around 1980.

Spanner

This term you might be most familiar with, since "spanner" is the British term for a wrench. It comes from the 17th Century and the German word "spannen" which was the tool used for winding the wheel lock of a firearm. It's also the origin of the phrase "spanner in the works" which means something that otherwise ruins one's plans.

White Spirit

While not exactly the same as paint thinner, white spirit the British term for mineral spirits, which are typically used to clean paint brushes and keep them getting gunked up with dried oil-based paints. Unlike paint thinner, mineral spirits don't have the same pungent aroma.

Breeze Block

Breeze block is a much cooler-sounding name for what Americans call a cinder block. The origins for the terms are very similar, as the blocks are commonly made from mixing concrete and ash, the latter of which is synonymous with the word "breeze" in Britain.

Stillson Wrench

Despite being an American invention, in America we call it a pipe wrench rather than giving it the name of its creator. Daniel C. Stillson invented the Stillson wrench in Massachusetts and the first patent on it was issued in 1869. Instead of naming it for Mr. Stillson, we gave it the name that follows its function, which is tightening or loosening pipe fittings.

Steel Rule

While we could call this a tape measure in America, in Britain that's used to refer to a tape measure that used by a tailor to take measurements for clothing. It gets the distinction by being made of a thin steel ribbon rather than cloth or plastic as is normal for the other kind of tape measure.

www.ingramcontent.com/pod-product-compliance
Lightning Source LLC
Chambersburg PA
CBHW081312070526
44578CB00006B/858

www.ingramcontent.com/pod-product-compliance
Lightning Source LLC
Chambersburg PA
CBHW081312070526
44578CB00006B/858